Biography
and
Autobiography

PRENTICE HALL
Upper Saddle River, New Jersey
Needham, Massachusetts

ISBN 0-13-437207-7

7 8 9 10   02 01

PRENTICE HALL

Acknowledgments

Grateful acknowledgment is made to the following for copyrighted material:

Atheneum Books for Young Readers, an imprint of Simon & Schuster Children's Publishing Division
From "I Want Some Sentimental Effusions of the Heart" from *Abigail Adams: Witness To A Revolution* by Natalie S. Bober. Copyright © 1995 by Natalie S. Bober. Reprinted by permission of Atheneum Books for Young Readers, an imprint of Simon & Schuster Children's Publishing Division.

Bantam Books, a division of Bantam Doubleday Dell Publishing Group, Inc.
From *Black Holes and Baby Universes and Other Essays* by Stephen W. Hawking. Copyright © 1993 by Stephen W. Hawking. Used by permission of Bantam Books, a division of Bantam Doubleday Dell Publishing Group, Inc.

Birch Lane Press
From *Rosie O'Donnell: Her True Story* by George Mair and Anna Green. Copyright © 1997 George Mair and Anna Green. Published by arrangement with Carol Publishing Group. A Birch Lane Press Book. Reprinted by permission of the publisher.

Chelsea House Publishers, a division of Main Line Book Co.
"Separate But Equal?" from *Barbara Jordan* by Rose Blue and Corinne Naden. Copyright © 1992 by Chelsea House Publishers. "First Wings" from *Amelia Earhart* by Nancy Shore. Copyright © 1987 by Chelsea House Publishers. Reprinted by permission of Chelsea House Publishers, a division of Main Line Book Co.

Doubleday, a division of Bantam Doubleday Dell Publishing Group, Inc.
From *Babe Didrikson* by Gene Schoor. Copyright © 1978 by Gene Schoor. Used by permission of Doubleday, a division of Bantam Doubleday Dell Publishing Group, Inc.

Enslow Publishing
From *Frida Kahlo: Portrait of a Mexican Painter* by Barbara C. Cruz. Copyright © 1996 by Barbara C. Cruz. Used by permission of Enslow Publishing.

(Acknowledgments continue on p. 154.)

Contents

Introduction

The word biography comes from two Greek words, *bios,* which means a *life,* and *graphien,* which means *to write.* The Greek form *auto* means *self.* Therefore, a biography is about someone else's life, and an autobiography is about the writer's own life.

Biography is one of the oldest forms of literature. Ancient records from Assyria, Babylonia, Egypt, and Greece include writings about the great kings and warriors, and the Bible contains many exciting life stories, such as those about David, Ruth, and Noah. Plutarch, the first-century philosopher who is considered the father of biography, described the lives of 46 Greek and Roman statesmen, rulers, and heroes so that others could follow their example.

Centuries later, biographers of the 1400's and 1500's became interested in their subjects as individuals rather than as role models. The Italian writer Vasari's biographies are still used as a source for learning about great artists such as Leonardo da Vinci and Michelangelo. In the 1700's, Benjamin Franklin wrote his famous *Autobiography,* which is still read today.

Biography became a highly popular form of literature during the 1800's. Biographers began to *interpret* the events in the lives of their subjects in addition to describing them. Authors offered their own perceptions about why people behaved in particular ways, so that two biographers writing about the same person might provide very different accounts of that person's life or character.

Today's biographers try to make their subjects human and interesting. They do a tremendous amount of research, sometimes spending literally thousands of hours reading books, letters, articles, and conducting interviews to gather information. Then they work to present the material in a lively, engaging style.

WHY DO WE READ BIOGRAPHIES?

You might wonder why people are so interested in reading about other people's lives, or why they might choose a biography over a novel. Below are just a few of the reasons that people read biographies.

INSPIRATION

Like people in ancient times, readers today enjoy knowing about positive examples—people who have shown unusual courage, generosity, or kindness. Readers can be inspired to act like them. Another possibility is that readers who are undergoing great difficulties, such as illness or grief, may find comfort and inspiration from reading biographies of people who have endured similar struggles. Biographies can give readers hope that they, too, can overcome their problems. In "My Experience with ALS," Stephen Hawking insists on living his life fully—exploring the study of advanced theoretical physics—despite what most of us would consider extreme physical limitations. In a selection from *Frida Kahlo: Portrait of a Mexican Painter,* Frida Kahlo teaches that one can overcome physical challenges and even use one's experience with pain to explore life and share it meaningfully with others through artistic expression. The essay "Separate but Equal?" describes Barbara Jordan, one of the great stateswomen of our time. She shares the basis for her strength and success, including her uncle's essential lesson that "Life is not a holiday but an education."

ENTERTAINMENT

Many historical and modern figures have led exciting lives, experienced narrow escapes, made astonishing discoveries, or simply found themselves in ridiculous situations. These biographies provide enjoyment because they are suspenseful, surprising, or just plain funny. In one of the selections in this book, "The Crown," Russell Baker provides an amusing and distinctly American perspective—along with a unique reporter's view—of the coronation of Queen Elizabeth of Great Britain. In another piece, Doris Kearns Goodwin relives her initiation into the world of television in a section from her book *Wait Till Next Year,* bringing us back to a time when television was not part of the common backdrop in the daily life of families.

INFORMATION

Biographies of well-known figures such as Nelson Mandela give readers a thorough understanding of their subjects, their personalities, and their historical importance. In "I Want Some Sentimental Effusions of the Heart," first lady Abigail Adams, a prolific letter-writer, eloquently combines everyday details and the living history of her tumultuous times. In "At Last I Kill a Buffalo," as Chief Luther Standing Bear describes the process of learning to kill a buffalo, he lets the reader feel the animals' thunderous power and the danger of the hunt.

CURIOSITY

Most people who have achieved success, wealth, or fame arouse our curiosity. We like to know that the celebrities we see in the movies or on television are human beings, not so different from ourselves. Like many others, Rosie O'Donnell wanted to be in show business for much of her young life. In an excerpt from *Rosie O'Donnell: Her True Story,* readers learn how she pursued her dream, serving as an example for others to follow. In the autobiographical *It's Always Something,* readers share Gilda Radner's discovery that humor is a powerful ally against the depression caused by a life-threatening illness.

Although biographies and autobiographies are categorized as *nonfiction,* they have much in common with a fictional story. Biographies have characters, settings, and a plot—and the people, places, and stories are all real. Reading these real stories teaches us that the lives of all of us—famous or not—contain moments of fascination that are not just interesting to others, but offer opportunities for learning more about how we might live.

Sisters, Brothers and Best Friends

La Familia

by Mary Helen Ponce

WHAT I most remember about my family was how different yet alike we all were. We ranged from tall to short, dark to light. And although I had no way of knowing what my first three siblings, Rosalía, Socorro, and Rito, had really looked like, I had four sisters and three brothers whom in some way I resembled.

Unlike those of our friends who looked Spanish, with light hair and green eyes, we looked like what we were: Mejicanos, with the coloring found among most people in Mexico. Yet our skin tones ranged from Nora's pale ivory to Ronnie's light olive and on down to Joey's dark olive. My skin was in between that of Ronnie and Elizabet: a medium olive with a yellow tinge.

Our eyes were mostly dark but all shaped differently. Nora's brown eyes were set far apart; in between was a pretty nose. Berney's hazel-green eyes turned a dark brown when he was angry. Elizabet had friendly brown eyes that twinkled when she smiled, which was often. Ronnie's eyes were a chocolate-brown rimmed in black and fringed with thick eyelashes. Trina's wide brown eyes were framed by black eyebrows that resembled birds' wings. My own eyes were neither as wide as Trina's nor as brown as Ronnie's. Josey had huge brown eyes that quickly filled with tears when he did not get his way.

We were tall, short, and in between. Nora, the eldest, was also the tallest of the girls. Elizabet and Ronnie were short-waisted (like our mother) and somewhat petite. Berney was tall and slender; Norbert was of medium height, with a muscular torso. Trina was tall and thin; I was tall and hefty. Josey was perfect.

Our handwriting was so similar! Berney, Norbert, and Josey all wrote the same squiggly letters, except that Norbert never misspelled a word. Nora's script was round, flowing, and graceful. Elizabet wrote in a delicate scrawl that was so like Nora's, except her L's weren't as round. Ronnie wrote almost like Elizabet and Nora, so that it was difficult for me to tell their notes apart. Trina's letters slanted to the right in graceful, round loops. Her P was fat, with a fancy curlicue at the beginning; she dotted her i's with a round, fat mark.

I learned to write using the Palmer method and slanted my letters to the right. Often they dropped off the page. I printed in block letters, but that took too long. Reluctantly I returned to cursive writing, intent on developing a distinctive style. But when I wasn't concentrating, I wrote just like my sisters.

Not only did the women in my family write alike, we all spoke in the same moderate voice. Just as my parents rarely raised their voices, I only learned to shout at Josey. Nora, a bit remote, never chatted, but talked only when she had to. Elizabet spoke in clear, concise paragraphs, while Berney would mumble his responses. Ronnie's voice was high and soft, like a dove cooing. She also whistled, a thing that irritated my brothers, who felt that only boys should know cómo chiflar.[1] Norbert sounded like a grown-up man when he talked. Trina and I inherited the same voice; we often even confused our parents. Josey whined like the spoiled brat he was; but his voice would rise to a deafening pitch when I rode his bike without permission.

We inherited straight teeth and small mouths. My father's teeth were tiny and straight, like a baby's milk teeth. Berney's teeth were larger than those of my father. Nora, Elizabet, and Ronnie had identical teeth and smiles. Norbert had large teeth, strong and white. Trina had bigger teeth than I did; her mouth was also wider. Josey and I had similar teeth. His mouth, I often thought, was more like that of a petulant girl's.

We were so alike, so different.

I was the tenth of eleven live children born to Tranquilino Ponce and Vicenta Solís. My mother miscarried twins, said to be boys, among her first five children. Of the first three—Rosalía, Socorro-the-First, and Rito—I only knew Rito, who died before I started school. And although my parents appeared not to dwell on their loss, they would allude now and then to their first years in this country and to the children they had lost. I thought of my first three siblings as *Them.*

Rosalía, or Rosalie as she was called in this country, was born in Mexico. My father, who came to this country at seventeen to join his older brothers, Felix and Gabriel, found work in the limoneras in Ventura. He saved his money and returned to Mexico. At twenty-two he married my mother, then twenty. They lived in Barretos, a ranch near León, Guanajuato, until about 1915, when my father decided to emigrate to this country for good. Once all their papers were in order, and with money sent them by my uncles in California, they left with Rosalía, their infant daughter. My mother often spoke of the trip and of having

---

1. **cómo chiflar:** how to whistle

to throw dirty diapers out the train windows because there was no place to put them. She hated to do it, something she felt was muy ranchero.[2] She waited until night fell, then threw the diapers out into the Arizona desert.

In a photograph taken when she was about thirteen, Rosalie looks tall for her age, tall and strong. Her hair is neither curly nor fashionable, but pulled back. She is wearing a plain cotton dress and dark shoes. I found it difficult to believe Rosalie was my sister, because she was so homely! She looked old for her age and terribly serious. I would stare and stare at the photo, trying to find a resemblance. I detected my mother's nose (hers too was flat, chata), but the eyes were different. I later learned that Rosalie had resembled Don Pedro Solís, my maternal grandfather. I also heard that when my mother, pregnant with me, visited Rosalie at Olive View Sanatorium (she later died of tuberculosis), Rosalía took one look at my mother's round belly and said, "Ay, pero para qué quiere más familia?"[3] I never heard my mother's response.

Rosalie died when I was three months old. The damp climate of las limoneras[4] settled in her lungs. She came down with tuberculosis, a disease prevalent among Mexican immigrants, and was quarantined, first at home, in los cuartitos,[5] the rooms my father and brothers occupied, then at a sanatorium. She died at eighteen.

María del Socorro, or Socorro-the-First as I thought of her, was born in Ventura, California. She was my parent's second child and lived but a short time. Her death was tragic and somewhat mysterious; I knew the details by heart. One day when she was about five, Socorro-the-First was playing with a boy from the labor camp. He had a box of matches and began to taunt her. The two chased each other around the camp. Suddenly he lit a match and threw it at her; her dress caught fire. Frightened of the flames that quickly enveloped her, she ran, not toward home but into the lemon groves! By the time my mother came to her rescue, Socorro-the-First was badly burned. She died a day later.

Although the boy had a reputation for being in trouble, his parents never acknowledged his part in the incident. Mis padres[6] forgave him and his parents, although my mother was devastated. My sister was buried in a simple plot somewhere in

---

2. muy ranchero: (colloq.) very uncivilized
3. "Ay, pero para qué quiere más familia?": "Oh, but why do you want more family?"
4. las limoneras: lemon groves
5. los cuartitos: little rooms
6. Mis padres: My parents

Ventura. Soon after that our family moved to Pacoima. When I first heard this story, I built up a hate for the boy and vowed to get him, but I never met him.

Rito, also born in Ventura, was my parent's first son; more than the others he resembled my father's family, most of whom had blue-green eyes. The one image I have of this brother, who died of tuberculosis right before World War II, is of a tall, slender man in pajamas! As a teenager sometime in the late 1930s, Rito, along with other young men from Pacoima, joined the Civilian Conservation Corps, called the CCC. He went off to dig ditches and work in the construction of roads. While there Rito caught frio; the cold settled in his lungs and developed into tuberculosis. He also spent the last years of his life at Olive View Sanatorium. Now and then he came home on a pass, but stayed alone in the cuartitos. He never ate with us; I don't remember him inside our house. Mostly he looked sad. Handsome and sad.

One day I had just finished my oatmeal and ran outside to play. Rito, then about twenty, was sitting alone in the back door of los cuartitos, in pajamas and slippers. He called me over and asked, "Why isn't your hair combed?" I put my hand to my curly hair, embarrassed at having Rito see me looking so messy. He pulled me to him, unpinned my barrette, and said, "go get a brush, and I will comb your hair." I did as he said, running past the kitchen and shouting at my startled mother, *"dónde 'sta el peine?"*[7] Comb in hand, I dashed outdoors again to where Rito awaited me. He sat me on his lap and began to unravel my messy hair. As he worked he spoke, his voice soft and low. "I don't like to see you with your hair in your face," he told me. "Always wash your face and comb your hair before going outdoors. Okay?"

I remember his touch, the long tapered fingers that gently separated my Shirley Temple curls, the blue-green eyes that looked into mine, the dark wavy hair that fell across his smooth white forehead. His sad look. Years later I developed a crush on actor Gilbert Roland (old even then). He reminded me of Rito, dear Rito, who by combing my messy hair had told me so much about himself.

Nora, baptized María-del-Socorro, was the eldest of our family as I knew it. She was given the same name as the sister who was burned, because it was said she looked like Socorro-the-First.

Nora had a certain air about her. Somewhat aloof and removed from the pack, she stood apart because of her height and

---

7. *"dónde 'sta el peine?"*: "Where's the comb?"

looks. Unlike the rest of us she was not olive-skinned at all, nor did she have a flat nose. She had beautiful creamy skin and large expressive eyes. She looked "international" and was often mistaken for Italian, Greek, or French.

Nora was an intellectual, a seeker of knowledge, a buyer of books. She learned from everyone and passed everything down to us. In high school she worked after school as a mother's helper for an Irish family in San Fernando and introduced us to peanut butter. She dropped out of school to work, which she later regretted. When she was eighteen, Nora was crowned Queen of the Pacoima Sixteenth of September fiesta, which made our father, a member of el comité,[8] very proud. She wore a white satin dress, a purple cape with a train, a rhinestone crown, and shoes bought for $2.99. She later worked as a live-in housekeeper for Helen Mack, a movie star of the thirties. There she learned about diet, hygiene, clothes, and makeup, as well as what she most tried to instill in us: good manners.

Her employer was generous; during Christmas, in addition to a bonus, she presented Nora with her old clothes: leather shoes, silk blouses, and also men's suits that fit my delighted father. One summer I was allowed to visit Nora for a week. I walked all around the pretty house and played in the garden with Miss Mack's son. All the while I pined for Josey and our pepper trees.

At the Macks' Nora acquired a taste for good hardwood furniture. She detested furniture in loud, gaudy colors, preferring muted tones that blended with everything. One piece at a time, paid for in cash, Nora bought most of what sat in our living room. The pretty hall table was brought home in my father's truck, wrapped in blankets.

I found it admirable that Nora did not spend all her hard-earned money on herself. Girls her age often spent their earnings on clothes, makeup, and ankle-strap shoes. Each Saturday they would take the bus to San Fernando to window-shop and try on the latest fashions. Nora did have pretty outfits, many of them given her by Miss Mack, and although she often missed Sunday mass, when she did attend (to please our mother) she looked lovely in print dresses and a wide picture hat with a large cabbage rose.

Nora had delicate hands. She rarely cooked but would now and then help make tortillas. She first removed her watch and

8. **el comité:** the committee

bracelets, then rinsed her hands in the bathroom and pinned her hair away from her face. She made perfectly round tortillas, light and fluffy, with nary a burned edge. I liked to watch her hands as they worked the rolling pin back and forth across the masa. Even when cooking, Nora was graceful.

Elizabet followed Nora. Unlike Nora, whom I associated with *Them,* Elizabet was part of the middle bunch: those who had come after Rito and lived. She was cheerful and industrious, and just as Nora did, loved our mother deeply. She emulated her in all things, never talked back, and was always willing to do more than her share of the housework.

Elizabet was my mother's right hand, a girl who helped with both the easy and hard chores. She cooked, cleaned, ironed. Anything and everything to earn our mother's favor. Elizabet, I think, suspected that Nora (said to be the spitting image of our maternal grandmother) was my mother's favorite, su preferida, although our mother would have denied it. Stuck between Nora-the-Beauty and Berney-the-First, Elizabet spent most of her life catering to our mother.

She was a fantastic cook and liked to improvise on old tested recipes. In grammar and high school she excelled in homemaking classes and learned to make pigs-in-a-blanket, hotcakes, and biscuits for us younger kids. She made rice pudding just the way I liked it, thick with cream and eggs, with cinammon sticks sticking out like matches. During Lent she helped toast the bread used to make capirotada, sweet bread pudding. She would cube the bread, add butter and brown sugar called piloncillo, crown this with raisins and cheese, then bake it in the oven. During Christmas she made delicious fudge. On hot summer days, Elizabet never seemed to tire of making pitchers of lemonade for her younger siblings.

She was also an expert seamstress. She knew everything about sewing: how to cut on the bias, adjust for fit, sew French seams, and add a sleeve gusset. She could turn a shirt collar and sleeve so that the material did not bunch up, followed sewing patterns to the letter, and rarely made mistakes when cutting out a dress. Best of all Elizabet knew how to make doll clothes. I thought her a genius!

Elizabet was also an excellent student. She did well in English and history, read voraciously, and acted as the family translator when necessary. She wrote letters to Mexico for our parents and explained instructions written in English to our father. In high school I once looked up Elizabet's report cards.

She had earned straight A's and not a single "Unsatisfactory."
She graduated with honors from San Fernando High School, the
first in our family to do so.

Elizabet was a bookworm; she read far into the night. Like me
she read Nora's Book of the Month Club selections and also
checked out books from the library in San Fernando. While
Nora stuck to the best-sellers, Elizabet liked historical novels
best, books she said had something called character. It was
Elizabet who bought me books each birthday and Christmas.
Nora made sure I had a winter coat; Elizabet bought dolls, buggies, and books.

By the time I was twelve, I was steeped in good literature and
had read *The Razor's Edge, Leave Her to Heaven,* and my favorite romance novel, *Came A Cavalier.* I rarely read *True Con-
fessions,* although Trina and I fought over *Photoplay.* These
were referred to as "garbage" by the learned Nora and studious
Elizabet. From an early age I could discern good literature from
trash. I never did care for comic books.

It was Elizabet who took me with her to choir practice when I
was eight years old. When the choir members, citing my young age,
objected to my singing with the adults, Elizabet merely smiled and
stood me next to her, holding the music book down low for me to
read. Later, when she no longer went to el coro, I continued on my
own. In many ways Elizabet was like my second mother; she set
the example for me in many things. I loved her dearly.

Elizabet was the first of her friends, all of whom aspired to
something other than a job in a ceramic plant or en el fil,[9] to
land a "good" job, in an attorney's office. As a business major in
high school, she had learned typing, shorthand, and account-
ing. During the early 1940s, girls yearned to be secretaries or
telephone operators, to work in an office, and to wear high heels
and white gloves. My parents were very proud of her.

No longer the disheveled teenager, Elizabet the "career girl"
wore pretty clothes, fashionable hats, and white gloves. One favorite outfit was a two-piece olive-green dress. The top was
polka-dotted, the skirt a swirl of neat pleats. The beige suit I
remember her wearing constantly was either her favorite or all
she had at the time. Always she wore white gloves, stockings
with seams, and leather pumps.

As a legal secretary Elizabet often accompanied her boss to
the Los Angeles county jail to take depositions. She remained at

---

9. en el fil: on the line

this job until World War II, when she, like others in Pacoima, went off to work in the aircraft plants, where the pay was good and women got to wear pants.

Elizabet worked on the assembly line at Lockheed Aircraft in Burbank, California. Like other Mexican-Americans on our street, she wanted to do her share in the war effort and to earn good money. She wore denim overalls and something called a snood, like a net but with bigger holes, wrapped around her dark head. On her tiny feet she wore the required safety shoes with closed toes and laces. These allowed her to work near machines; the pants let her bend over.

Nora and Elizabet both paid my mother for room and board. Elizabet still cooked, but not as much. My mother felt that she should not have to work both at the plant and at home. And then Elizabet fell from grace; she eloped with R., a handsome young man who wore a snappy uniform.

During the war everyone in town thought of eloping. Couples met in the middle of the night, then drove to Tijuana, Las Vegas, or Mexicali to get hitched, something that drove our pastor crazy. He felt that everyone should marry en la iglesia,[10] having taken instruction and announced their marriage bans. I never got the details about Elizabet's dash to the altar, but I recall that my parents were disappointed and hurt. Up to that time, she had done no wrong. I found it terribly exciting. Almost like in the movies, except that there a girl would climb down a ladder from an upstairs window into the waiting arms of her novio,[11] then off they went to get hitched by a judge. I was curious to know what Elizabet had worn and where they went for a honeymoon, but no one bothered to tell me. Later Elizabet did get married en la iglesia; otherwise the whole town would say they were living in sin. Not until her husband was discharged and they rented a small house on Carl Street, did she have children.

I went to Elizabet's every single day! She always made me feel welcome. I liked to see and touch the things most newlyweds bought: the new iron, shiny toaster, chrome table with matching chairs, and the pretty flowered sheets and taffeta bedspread. Elizabet now had a portable sewing machine on which to make curtains, tablecloths, and pillow shams.

10. en la iglesia: in the church
11. novio: boyfriend

I never could make up my mind whom I most wanted to be like: Elizabet or Nora. I admired Nora's cool beauty, good taste, and regal bearing, but always felt good around Elizabet; she was always there. When I was about ten I decided to be like both my eldest sisters, to take bits of Elizabet and combine them with Nora's attributes.

Berney, my eldest brother, was two years younger than Elizabet. This was hard to believe, because she appeared to defer to him. After Rito died, Berney, still a teenager, readily assumed the authoritarian role and privileges of el hijo mayor.[12] He was tall, with hazel green eyes, a straight nose, and perfect white teeth. His black hair was wavy, kinky almost. People said he resembled my father and that he was almost as handsome as Rito. Unlike my father, however, Berney was often grumpy; yet his face lit up when he smiled, his hazel eyes crinkling at the corners. He was neither as friendly as Norbert nor as sweet as Josey (no one was as sweet as Josey), but was a typical older brother who liked to give orders. Being the responsible, older male in the family made Berney serious, I often thought. He was terribly neat and often changed tee shirts twice a day, a thing that delighted my mother, who like others on Hoyt Street, hated for her children to be called "dirty Mexicans." She would in fact boil our clothes for hours. Years later I met my mother's brother, Benjamin, in Mexico and recognized Berney's face and disposition.

Sometimes when Josey and I got into his tools, Berney would growl and threaten to hit us; at other times he would sweetly offer to take us to town.

"Ya wanna go?"

"Where?"

"You don't havta know."

"But . . ."

"Get in the truck and wait for me."

Josey and I, excited at the prospect of riding with our older brother, would quickly scramble into our father's flatbed truck to sit and wait. And wait. When finally we would climb down from the dusty truck, it was only to discover that Berney had taken off in his car, leaving us behind. This happened at least once a week, with Josey and me none the wiser.

Like my father, Berney was a fixer of broken things. He faithfully worked on his old jalopy, a dented Ford, called "el foringo," held together with loving care and bailing wire and washed at

12. **el hijo mayor:** the oldest son

least once a week. He staked out a corner of the garage for himself and would stay in there for hours. Before working on his car, Berney would put on old Levis and a worn tee shirt, then borrow my father's work shoes, not wanting to smear his cordovan shoes with oil. He would sweep the area clean, then lay down pieces of cardboard to catch the oil that oozed from the car motor. Then, my father's tool box at his side, Berney would go to work. He yanked at loose wires, wound electrical tape around a torn hose, replaced spark plugs and points. Berney I often thought, could fix anything.

But Berney had one bad habit. When he was working on a car and found himself in need of rags for his oily hands, rather than getting up and hunting for rags underneath the kitchen sink, he would grab at whatever was hanging on the clothesline. This irritated my mother, who more often than not kept the lines filled with our clothes. She was forever scolding Berney, who more than once had ruined towels, pillowcases, and once a lace doily.

Ay, pero qué hiciste?[13] my mother would ask Berney. "What have you done to my doily?"

"What doily? Ya mean this rag?"

One time I hand washed my favorite doll's dress in the kitchen sink. The pink dress of light gossamer, had lace at the bottom, tiny pearl buttons at the back, and underneath, a slip of white taffetta. I hung the dress to dry on the line, unaware that Berney was then working on his car. When I returned for the dress later, I found it streaked with oil. Berney, I suspected, had wiped the dipstick on my doll's dress, and then had hung it back on the line. I ran screaming to Doña Luisa, our next-door neighbor and adopted grandmother. Rather than show disrespect for her, Berney retreated under his car. Whenever Berney, and later Norbert, was working on a car, my mother tried to be sure to bring in the wash.

Berney liked to throw his weight around at home. He felt responsible for my sisters' reputations. He disapproved of the tight skirts then in vogue, and although Elizabet was older, she was too short to have much authority. Even Norbert rarely argued with the brother who had a car and could outshout him. Berney was not mean, nor did he hit us (in our house, no one was allowed to hit), but in our mother's eyes he could do no wrong. To make Berney angry was to incur our mother's

---

13. **Ay, pero qué hiciste?:** Oh, but what did you do?

coraje. Doña Luisa called Berney "el pádre";[14] she all but curt-
sied to him. Berney never talked back to our parents, although
he rebelled against them when he quit high school to get a job.
He was never a pachuco[15] (what parents in Pacoima most
feared), but sometimes, when my father wasn't looking, he
wore draped pants that ballooned around his slender frame.

My older sisters stayed clear of Berney. Still Berney always
knew where they went and with whom.

Berney came of age during the war, a time when most guys
were raring to leave the barrio[16] to "fight Japanese." Many of
Berney's buddies signed up with the army, navy, Seabees, and
marines, choosing not only a branch of the military but also a
uniform to wear. In the army, men led the charge; Seabees built
airstrips and bridges; marines secured the front lines. Sailors
traveled more than the others and wore snappy white hats. For
Mexican-Americans with an eighth-grade education and few
prospects, the war offered excitement, a steady job, and adventure.

Many of our neighbors on Hoyt Street volunteered for the
draft. Friends and brothers drove to Los Angeles in beat-up cars
to enlist, hoping to be assigned to the same outfit. On our street
kids bragged about brothers in the service, arguing over who
wore the neatest uniform. The marine dress uniform, white
gloves included, won hands down.

Poor Berney. When war broke out, he was about eighteen. He
too wanted to fight for his country, so he signed up with the
army. During the physical his hearing was found to be defective
because of a burst ear drum (the result of childhood ear infec-
tions); he was classified as 4-F. His dream of fighting in the war
alongside his friends ended.

In the barrio being 4-F was akin to a disgrace and somewhat
suspect, because many men, especially those who feared getting
shot, used any and all afflictions to evade the draft. Some fled to
Mexico to live with relatives, others claimed they were the sole
support of their mothers.

Berney had to endure the hard stares of those who did not
know of his affliction. Wanting to contribute to the war effort, he
went to work for Lockheed-Vega, the aircraft company in Burbank where Elizabet also worked.

---

14. "el pádre": "the father"
15. pachuco: a punk
16. barrio: neighborhood

I defended Berney to my friends. When they questioned his being at home rather than fighting, I stood tall, daring anyone to call my brother a coward. Yet he must have been very lonely, because during the war, the barrio, especially Hoyt Street, was empty of young, virile men.

My mother and Doña Luisa were perfectly content to have Berney sit out the war; they had no need to worry about his being wounded or killed. It was better to have him be alive than to have a gold star on a windowpane. My father, who understood everything, said nothing. After having lost three children, he no longer questioned fate. But I think Berney did.

Verónica, or Ronnie, followed Berney in birth order; after Elizabet moved away, she took over her side of the bed. Nora had left her job with Helen Mack and was working for Timms Aircraft; she had her own apartment.

Like Elizabet Ronnie was short, but she resembled my father. She had chocolate-brown eyes, a tiny mouth, and (unlike Elizabet, who had the Solís nose) her aristocratic nose jutted out from her heart-shaped face. Her widow's peak was shown to advantage when she brushed back her thick dark hair. She had a tiny waist, full hips and short, skinny legs. She kept her toes painted a bright pink.

Ronnie was an obedient daughter who never talked back to our parents. She was said to be my father's favorite, which she also believed. She was easy to get along with, easy to know. Unlike the rest of us, Ronnie was not a reader and rarely discussed anything other than clothes. She was not as knowledgeable as Elizabet or Nora, but she was friendly, pretty, and popular.

All of my sisters were extremely generous, Ronnie more than the others. At the church bazaars, jamaicas, she would give Josey and me money to spend on popcorn and peanuts. At Christmas she would pitch in to buy dolls for me and toys for Josey.

Ronnie never did much housework, a thing that irked Trina. Unlike Elizabet, who was always cleaning and cooking, Ronnie, backed by our doting mother, delegated the dirty chores to Trina and me. When Ronnie did cook, the menu was predictable: meat loaf, mashed potatoes, and green peas. She rarely deviated from this, nor did she experiment with recipes, but now and then she fixed a carrot-and-raisin salad. Mostly she kept busy moving furniture around.

Ronnie was the artist in the family. In high school she was encouraged by her art teacher to major in art. She worked well with every medium: charcoal, pen and ink, and watercolors, but she was especially good with oils. Her paintings were exhibited in school, much to the delight of our mother, who unfortunately never saw them.

Ronnie was also an expert at arranging flowers. She instinctively knew which flowers went well together. She preferred tall, stately varieties: gladiolus, iris, and calla lilies. She trimmed the leaves, then stuck the blossoms inside a "frog," an iron dish with spikes. Around them she arranged ferns or other greens. We always had fresh flowers in our house.

In our family it was said that artistic abilities came from the Solis side, intellect from the Ponces. Although Ronnie looked like the Ponces, she was very creative. She was constantly moving our furniture around, never quite satisfied with her surroundings. She would group pictures together and sew pretty cushions for our faded sofa. Unlike Elizabet, who wore tailored clothes, or Nora, who liked print dresses, Ronnie doted on peasant skirts, which she whipped up on our mother's trusty sewing machine. She wore them with frilly white blouses of batiste or cotton. One of her favorites was a white eyelet blouse worn off the shoulders.

In high school Ronnie was exempt from much of the housework. From the time she was sixteen, she worked part-time as an usherette at the San Fernando Theater and was in fact the first Mexican-American girl hired there. She worked after school and on weekends and would allow no one to loiter in the theater aisles. Most evenings my father picked her up.

Ronnie was flirtatious but sensible. She had a lot of boyfriends, many of them Berney's friends, who hung around our house. She took care with whom she dated and rarely stayed out late. Ronnie did not want to disappoint the parents whose expectations of her knew no bounds. Of all the girls in our family, only Ronnie had a big wedding; apart from working at a factory job, that was all a Mexican girl could aspire to at the time.

After high-school graduation in the 1940s, Ronnie attended Los Angeles City College on an art scholarship. She would take the bus from San Fernando Road to the city. She rarely talked about her classes, but appeared to like being una artista. Within a year she decided she should earn money, however, and quit college. I think she felt guilty about not helping out at home.

All of my older siblings contributed at home. Early on Nora set the example for taste and generosity. She bought Easter bonnets and frilly dresses for Trina and me and rompers for Josey, as well as much of the family furniture. Elizabet helped buy a stove and washing machine for our mother. Berney and Ronnie also gave mi mamá a portion of their earnings, not so much as room and board but out of respect. This was common in the barrio, where those who worked usually helped their parents with money.

Years later, when our mother was seriously ill, Ronnie (then married and working outside the home) gave my father her weekly salary to pay for the private hospital where my mother was confined. She was following the example set by my father; when Rosalía and Rito were en el sanatorio, he mortgaged our home to pay for the medical treatment.

I never went anywhere with Ronnie. She had her own set of friends and could not be bothered with a pesky kid sister. We shared few things, other than the moving of furniture (I was hefty and liked to push). Ronnie was of the World War II generation and experienced fully the new freedoms given young women at that time. She, Elizabet, and Nora went to dances given at el Salón Parra as part of the war effort. Encouraged by our new progressive priest, they invited soldados to the church bazaars that soon teemed with men in uniform. Dark-eyed sailors and soldiers flirted with my sisters; I envied them their newfound freedom.

Ronnie never worked in an aircraft company. By the time she left college, most airplane factories were laying off workers. She got a job at Gladding, McBean & Company, a ceramic factory in Glendale where few if any Mexican-Americans worked. She was hired because she had an artistic background and could hand paint the dishes the company was famous for. She helped many of her friends find work there, too. In 1949 she married a handsome sailor and moved to a small town southeast of Pacoima.

Trina and I aspired to have a house like Ronnie's. Although her first house was small, she and her husband built and paid for it piece by piece. They then built two more, each one larger than the last, and finally settled into the prettiest one, a custom-made house with pegged floors, wide shutters, and pretty wallpaper. We admired the beautiful maple furniture in the bedrooms, lamps, coffee tables, the refrigerator, the freezer, and the outdoor barbeque. Each time I visited Ronnie, I took inventory to see what was new. None of her friends equalled Ronnie's material gains; she had everything.

Norbert was born after Ronnie. Like Elizabet, he had a flat nose, chato. He was not as handsome as Berney nor as rambunctious as Josey, but he was kind and sensitive. During the war he was still in high school, so he did not get to play soldier. He read a lot but did not frequent the library or snitch books from Nora. Norbert was short and husky; his terrific build was due to weight lifting.

He and his friends, guys he called "my buddies," wore tight Levis and white tee shirts and spent hours fixing jalopies passed down to them by an older brother. Norbert worked well with his hands; he loved to fiddle with car engines, carburetors, and fuel pumps. At supper Josey and I sat across from Norbert, who as I recall never had to sit on the bench with the kids; because he was un hombre,[17] he got a chair.

Norbert preferred animals to people. He also had a fascination with names and even wrote his name on my father's truck. He wrote it as Norbt., a peculiar abbreviation, and also as Norb or Bert, but never as Norbert.

As a teenager he worked for O'Meara of the Valley, a landscape gardener who would pick him up each Saturday morning. He knew all about plants and how they grew best: in sandy or rich soil, sun or shade. Once instead of wages, Norbert brought home a Chinese willow tree.

The day Norbert brought home the weeping willow tree was terribly exciting. He ran in, eyes shining, hair tousled, to tell my father he had a Chinese tree for the front yard. As Josey and I watched, Norbert and my father unloaded the tree, taking care not to disturb the roots encased in burlap. They sat the tree down, then Norbert grabbed the garden hose and drenched it, saying that providing it got plenty of water, anything could grow. Even polliwogs.

Norbert walked around the yard, his Levis caked with dirt, trying to decide where to plant the tree. He inspected the back, side, and front yards, rubbing his curly head, unable to make up his mind. Now and then he sunk the hoe into the ground as if testing the soil. Finally he decided the willow would look best in the front yard, a little to the right of center. Supervised by my father, Norbert dug a hole.

"Así?"[18]

"No, más grande."[19]

I watched as he dug the hole with the square shovel. Once he had a grip on the handle, his hands never shifted, or else they might get callouses. As Norbert worked, our dog, Duke, ran be-

17. **un hombre:** a man
18. **"Así?":** "Like this?"
19. **"No, más grande.":** "No, bigger."

tween his legs, excited at having another tree to pee on.

"Gosh, Josey, no one else has a Chinese willow."

"In the whole world?"

"No, stupid. They gots them in . . ."

"China?"

Often Josey exasperated me with his questions. When I wasn't looking he would read my schoolbooks and scribble his answers to math problems in my writing tablet. He beat me at marbles and wanted a *World Book Encyclopedia* to show he could memorize things better than I could. As we watched Norbert, Josey paid close attention; should I ever plant anything, bury an ant even, Josey would be ready to instruct me.

By late afternoon Norbert was ready for the tree. He wet the roots again, then slowly lifted the tree and placed it in the gaping hole. My father was concerned that the precious tree not grow lopsided; he held it ramrod straight as Norbert filled the hole. His muscular arms gleaming with sweat, his face damp with excitement, Norbert then turned the hoe upside down and punched holes around the roots to let the air escape. Finally he made a watering trench around the tree that from afar resembled Elizabet's pie crusts.

My father watched as Norbert added a concoction, given him by O'Meara of the Valley, to keep the tree from going into shock, then walked off, satisfied with Norbert's handiwork.

The tree was beautiful; its moss-green leaves swept to the ground. That evening my friends on Hoyt Street came by to see it.

"Gosh! Did it really come from China?"

"No stupid, from a can."

"Shut up."

"You gonna make me?"

For a time the tree thrived, then little by little it began to shed its leaves. The slender branches turned brown. Poor Norbert didn't know what to do. He watered it even more, added fertilizer and vitamins, but still the tree drooped, its once green branches now dry and brittle. Mr. O'Meara came by to give advice. He snapped a tiny branch off the tree, looked at it, then shook his head. Soon the tree died.

A broken-hearted Norbert dug up the tree and carted it to the back; just before he dumped it in the trash, he inspected its roots. Later my father said the tree had rotted from too much water. Soon after, my father brought home a palm tree. Norbert pitched in to plant it, although compared to the Chinese willow, the palm was ugly and added nothing to the yard. I hated this tree and secretly hoped it would go the way of the willow, but it survived.

Another time Norbert brought home a pretty cocker spaniel. Eyes full of happiness, dog clutched tight against his chest, he placed it at our feet. I picked up the yapping, squirming bundle of caramel fur. Josey too latched onto the dog, although we both knew he was Norbert's special pet and not a replacement for el Duque, who had recently died. Norbert, who took his time about most things, did not immediately name the dog; he thought and thought about it. He wanted something that fit the dog's personality. Josey and I offered suggestions: Spot, Brownie, Perro. Norbert shook his head. He named the dog several times, then changed his mind. Worried that this dog might join the long line of Duques, he finally named the taffy-colored dog Fawn. A perfect name, pretty and poetic. He bought the dog a collar, then sat in the warm sun to brush its fur. He was always happy around Fawn.

Norbert joined the air force while I was still in grammar school. He signed up, he said, because the air force guaranteed him an education. Although he was one semester from high-school graduation, he refused to wait. I often felt that Norbert, the most intelligent of my brothers, wanted something more than Pacoima had to offer; he wanted to do things, to see the world.

Norbert spent two years in Munich, Germany, where he learned to speak German and made master sergeant. In his letters (which I read aloud to our mother), he explained that if he were married, he would qualify for off-base housing. I understood only that he was enjoying himself and seeing something of the world.

As the family's official letter writer (now that Elizabet was gone), I wrote Norbert long, chatty letters. I liked to write, and since I was willing, my mother asked me to write on her behalf. In his brief letters Norbert sent photos of the pretty *fräuleins* he met in Munich.

Once after not hearing from Norbert for almost a month, my mother was in a near panic. She consulted Elizabet (everyone consulted Elizabet), who suggested that we get in touch with the Red Cross. A few weeks later we received a bundle of letters from Munich. Much later, when Norbert came home, he told us about his embarrassment and anger when he was instructed by the company commander to "Write home, now!"

Mostly Norbert wrote to me. One Christmas he sent me a German radio and camera in a fancy case. When the postman delivered the cardboard box I ran outside, grabbed a pair of pliers, and tore at it, but was called inside. Just then a friend of my father's drove up and smashed the box, which was lying in the driveway. The radio was now a jumble of wires and tubes; the shiny camera though, was untouched.

The camera, a Zeiss-Ikon was perfect! It had numerous dials and settings for distance and height and a thick, wide lens. I learned to photograph moving objects by setting the camera for 0/seconds, bought rolls of black-and-white film at the corner store, then took pictures of everyone and everything. I carried my camera to school and to the beach. I could identify the detailed pictures taken by my Zeiss-Ikon; I had a fit when Trina snitched photos I knew came from my camera. I charged the film and development at the market, where Maggie, a friendly girl, wrote out receipts for the purchase of stewing beef. When my mother found out, I took the film elsewhere. I had the German camera for years; it was my most precious possession.

When he returned from Germany, Norbert drove me nuts with the foreign words and expressions he had picked up. He no longer said "hi!" but what sounded like *vee-gates.* He called Josey and me *dumkoffs,* swine even! My parents became *Frau* and *Herr* Ponce; my sisters *fräuleins.* He sang American songs in German, too, his eyes twinkling with merriment as Josey and I listened in awe. When Josey and I fought, Norbert would come between us, saying: "At ease." I think he missed military life—and Germany.

After Norbert came Trina, a tall, girl who resembled Berney. Although we were only three years apart, the distance between us was great, because from the time I was three, I slept next door with Doña Luisa. We never got to know each other. We neither shared dolls, buggies, or secrets.

Trina was moody and difficult to like. She hated catechism and the nuns, gave not a whit for Girls Scouts, nor cared to sing in the church choir. Although she was a good student and brought home A's, we never did homework together. I didn't know how to act around this sister.

There was little for Trina to aspire to. Caught between the popular Ronnie and a kid sister who was gaining on her, she did not aim to please. Nora was the family beauty, Elizabet had the brains, and Ronnie was *una artista.* Trina had a hard act to follow.

My sister Trina, I often thought, was caught up in the many

changes that followed the end of war, a time when everything seemed to change: clothes, hairdos, cars, and attitudes. Trina and her friends criticized their parents for being "old fashioned" (later I did, too). They made fun of Mexican dichos[20] and traditions, chewed wads of gum, and drooled over "cool cats" who were "hep to the jive." Few parents in our town understood the needs of these new teenagers who yearned to be like the girls in the movies, las Americanas in tight skirts and cardigan sweaters who spent hours listening to music. On screen teenagers drank and acted tough. The guys wore tight Levis and cussed a blue streak. They didn't give a hoot about what parents thought. Popular songs were terribly suggestive and urged kids to rebel. Parents who could not control their teenagers called them mal agradecidos[21] with no respect for God or their parents. If a girl came home past midnight, she was said to be bad, bad enough to be sent to juvenile hall.

Our pastor preached against the new ideas and new freedoms. He abhorred the tight skirts worn by girls like Trina, calling them disgraceful. He felt they could only lead to occasions of sin. He frowned on modern dance styles, too, claiming there was nothing wrong with the waltz, which allowed room for a book to pass between the dancers (his way of measuring a proper distance). He hated teen jargon and cringed when he heard "cool cat," "hep to the jive," and "all reet-tweet."

It was as teenagers that Trina and I bonded. Once I left Doña Luisa to live full-time with the family (at the age of twelve or so), we shared a bedroom and giggled far into the night. We wore the same size clothes and shoes; we shared plaid skirts, pastel sweaters, and saddle oxfords. Often Trina talked me into letting her wear my new clothes. When later my friends commented on my sister's new sweater, I would have a fit, insisting the sweater was really mine. We scrutinized movie magazines for beauty secrets and spent our money on Max Factor pancake makeup (#2), Tangee lipstick, Maybelline, and rouge. Now and then we went to town together, but once there Trina would take off with her friends.

One summer night Trina and I went to a beach party at Zuma Beach, the "in" place among teenagers. We packed bathing suits, towels, and makeup, then met our friends near the corner. We got home past midnight. The back door was locked; Trina and I climbed in through the kitchen window. Just as I

20. dichos: sayings; proverbs
21. mal agradecidos: ungrateful

brought my knees up to the window sill, Berney drove in. With Trina pulling I jumped, scraping my legs on the floor. I limped to bed, while she secured the window. Minutes later Berney barged inside and peeked into the bedroom, where Trina and I, still in our wet suits, pretended to be sleeping. Later Berney hid Trina's favorite skirt, the one with the slit up the side. He stuck it behind a closet, but I found it and gave it back to her. When Berney saw her in the dreaded skirt, he frowned, once more acting like the older brother.

To my family I was Nena. Not María Elena or Mary Helen, but Nena, Nanny-goat, Nena-llorona, and what only my father called me, Malena. Although I liked my Spanish name, I was never attached to it. While my friends and I spoke Spanish all the time, we liked our names in English best, never questioning teachers who, rather than struggle with our "foreign" names, quickly deduced their American counterparts and entered them on our school records. In time we identified only with our names in English and even forgot how to spell our Spanish names.

Not even Doña Luisa, who spoke only en español, called me by my proper name, mi nombre propio. Father Mueller once said my French name was Marie Hélène, which sounded pretty, but so did María Elena. When the Mexican waltz "María Elena" (translated into English from the Spanish) became popular, I identified with the romantic lyrics, but this affectation did not last. I was never María Elena.

I was called "la llorona," crybaby, because I liked to cry. I would cry at least once a day. I cried when my brothers threatened to tease me, cried harder when they prepared to tease me, and screamed in earnest when they did tease me. Doña Luisa, exasperated at my continuous wailing, said that if I continued to cry my eyes would shrink. Se te van a cerrar los ojos, she argued, her voice hoarse and cross.

I began to examine my eyes in the bathroom mirror, peering closely at the pupils. With my index finger I measured the length of each eye, then compared measurements. Thinking they might shrink too, I began to measure my eyelids. Once in a photo my eyes resembled two slits. I stopped crying for a whole week. But I missed this form of expression and soon began crying again for any and all reasons.

Crying was something girls did. In the movies, including those shown at the church hall, women who cried got their way. Teary teenage girls were never spanked, but only sent to their room with a glass of warm milk. Husky cowboys fell apart at the sight of a girl in tears. In Mexican movies tough hombres were themselves moved to tears by those of their novias and mamacitas.[22] Even big brothers like Berney gave in to sniveling siblings who wore Shirley Temple curls.

But I was a real professional and soon had an entire repertoire of wails. At church, especially on Good Friday, I sobbed along with Doña Luisa and the Trinidads, three viejitas[23] whom my friends and I considered religious fanatics. When I began to whimper in my pew, Doña Luisa quickly put her thin arms around me; by the time mass was over, I knew she would buy me my favorite sweets.

As la llorona of the family, crying got me out of numerous scrapes and household chores. If we were playing ball and I felt cheated, I cried in short, loud gasps, then took the ball and went home. I cried buckets when forced to accompany Ronnie to church against my will and screeched at Trina when she locked me out of the bathroom. Each time I didn't get my way, I first checked to see who was around, then took a deep breath and hit high C.

Josey, two years younger than I, was my favorite playmate. He had dark brown eyes, a tiny mouth, and hair that shone blue-black in the California sun. He was said to resemble our father, except that he was dark, muy moreno.

He was terribly spoiled. As the baby of the family, he was my older sisters' plaything. Like royalty, he was carried aloft while I followed at ten paces. Mis hermanas[24] would parade him up and down the street as if he were a rare jewel. They tossed him in the air, smoothed his hair, tweaked his nose, and cooed in his ear, while I kicked at dirt clods.

As el más chiquito,[25] Josey was kept spotless by our doting mother and Doña Luisa, who, when she looked at Josey, appeared to be seeing God. Once he was scrubbed clean and his hair brushed off his face, Josey was dressed in starched rompers and high-tops. He would follow me around the yard, rarely more than a few feet away. We would hold hands or chase each other, while Doña Luisa watched us from afar. We made up songs, dug holes, and climbed the walnut tree. I was his leader; Josey was my follower.

---

22. novias and mamacitas: girlfriends and dear mothers
23. viejitas: little old ladies
24. Mis hermanas: My sisters
25. el más chiquito: the smallest

Together Josey and I explored the open field, el llano. We rolled in the moist carpet of grass extending the length of the lot and scraped our knees on protruding rocks. We poked at the numerous insects that lived here. Josey liked ladybugs but feared moscos; we would quickly return to the safety of our own yard. We ran circles around the pepper trees, los pirules. Now and then we would stray to the street to play with other kids, but we liked each other's company best. What I liked the most about Josey was that he obeyed orders: "Josey, get the ball," "Josey, gimme the bat." He always obeyed without complaining.

Josey was highly intelligent; in grammar school he was moved up not one, but two years! I feared he would pass me up; hoping to spot a mistake, I would watch carefully as he worked a math problem. He and I rarely fought. "I'm older and bigger," I pointed out. As he grew older, the dusky skin that in summer turned blue-black began to bleach out, but his hair, with nary a wave, remained thick and straight.

Josey was musical. Elizabet had once played the violin and Berney played a mean harmonica, but Josey had the better ear. He would memorize all the songs sung by the Andrew Sisters and he knew the name of every band, bandleader, and instrument played. He was forever tapping his fingers to an imaginary beat; he knew the difference between two-four, three-four, and four-four time. Once he learned to read music, he memorized scales, musical notes, and words like *fortissimo, allegretto,* and *pianissimo.* When he was about twelve, my father bought him a shiny saxaphone and drove him to San Fernando each week for music lessons.

Every day Josey practiced el saxofón. He began with scales, then attacked the lesson of the week. Up and down the scale he would go, his dark eyes bulging, his cheeks puffed out like a cobra's. He liked to rip, as he called the spurts of sound emitting from the sax. He discovered jazz. When he heard a familiar tune on the radio, Josey would grab his sax and rip along, never missing a beat. When he was done with a lesson, Josey polished the shiny instrument, then placed it in its coffin. He later got a music stand and a metronome. Once he found his calling, Josey quit playing ball in the street. If forced to he would help to field the ball, but he much preferred to fiddle with the saxaphone. He later formed a band that played at his high school prom. For years our house was filled with the sound of jazz.

Ours was a well-organized household. Because we were a large family and our parents liked to keep us busy and out of trouble, we were each allocated jobs according to our size and capabilities. Grumbling but respectful, we went about our work, intent on pleasing our parents, whose concern with cleanliness and order was evident in everything they did.

Saturdays were special. En nuestra familia[26] each person had special chores on this day. While my mother boiled linens or ironed, all of us except for Nora would go about our work. (On Saturdays Nora slept late. As a "career girl" who worked long hours during the week, she was exempt from the usual, boring housework.)

Elizabet would retreat to the kitchen to concoct new recipes from scratch. She began with what was at hand, then improvised. Invariably she left dirty pots in the sink.

Ronnie's Saturday job was to sort and fold linens: sheets, pillowcases, and towels fresh from the clothesline. She would stack them in the hall closet as I watched, curious to see whether she folded towels as neatly as Nora or I. Ronnie could be as neat as a pin—providing she felt like it. Often she cared not a whit whether the sheets lay straight or not, but finished the job in record time. Saturday was also Ronnie's day to iron her school clothes.

En los sabados[27] Trina cleaned the bathroom, grumbling as she scrubbed the tub, washbowl, and toilet seat. She would lock the door and turn up the radio she had hidden in the hamper while I pounded on the bathroom door. She would take her hidden makeup and slather it on her face. When she emerged at long last, the bathroom would be spotless, her eyes caked with Maybelline.

Josey, still coddled by everyone, would help my father outdoors. He swept leaves with the yardbroom, whose handle kept falling off. Josey mostly ran errands for the rest of us. "Josey, hand me the hammer, traeme el martillo." "Josey, you gotta go to the store." Josey was our little helper, providing we later rewarded him with his favorite candy.

My Saturday job was to dust, shampoo, and polish the six dining room chairs. I had this job for about three years and hated it for all of them, because it had bypassed my sisters. "Trina never did them," I complained to my mother. Each Saturday before I could attend catechism or play with my friends, I first had to clean all six chairs. All six! Perfectly, shiny, clean.

---

26. En nuestra familia: In our family
27. En los sabados: On Saturdays

The chairs were of dark mahogany, upholstered in beige and maroon flowers. Four of the chairs had straight-backs; two had arms. Since our house lacked a dining room and a dining table, las sillas were used as occasional chairs in the living room; two were stuck in the hall. The somber-looking chairs were much too elegant for the kitchen, Nora insisted. Josey and I were not allowed to use them at supper; we continued to sit on the bench.

On Saturday mornings soon after breakfast, I prepared for the dreaded chore. I placed old newspapers on the porch floor, then took flannel squares (cut from old pajamas) from the rag bag under the kitchen sink; they absorbed the furniture oil and did not scratch the wood. The small brush used to scrub the chair seats was also kept under the kitchen sink, with a round pan. Once armed with the necessary tools, I was ready for the chairs.

I would lug the chairs to the porch, holding them aloft so as not to scratch the wood, set them down, then return for the rest. Using short, swift strokes, I brushed the dust off each chair; when I was finished I lined the chairs against the porch rail to inspect them for stains. Then in a small bowl I mixed furniture shampoo with water. I whipped the suds to a thick foam, then before they dissipated, I carried the foam-filled dish outside and placed it on the newspaper.

Next came the fun parts! I swished the brush back and forth in the shampoo, then cleaned the chairs with the foam. I swiped at the beige and maroon design, using the short strokes Nora had taught me, being careful not to soak the chairs. When I was satisfied that the chairs were clean of stains, I emptied the dregs in a nearby bush.

Once the chairs were dry, I took a soft cloth and saturated it with Old English Furniture Polish. I turned the chairs upside down, then went to work. My hands wound around each chair leg; I rubbed and rubbed, then attacked the back and sides. Then I went to find Nora. If she agreed that the chairs were finished, I carried them back to their designated rooms. If not, I pushed them against the porch and, after catechism, did them over again. And hated it.

On Saturday we also prepared for Sunday. After I returned from catechism—and providing the chairs were done—I changed the bed linens. Elizabet, whose job this had once been, had taught me how. "Open the windows to let out los malos humores, dust the mattress, and change both sheets. Turn the ends under, or you'll have a lumpy bed."

As I grew older my Saturday jobs also included cleaning the cuartitos, a job I relished because it allowed me to pry into my brother's dresser drawers. I read the instruction booklets sent by Charles Atlas that Norbert kept hidden in a drawer. His dirty clothes were scattered all over the floor; Berney's white tee shirts sat in a neat pile. When I finished with the sheets, I would lie down on Berney's bed.

When Saturday rolled around once more, our family again went about our assigned chores. I would clean the detested chairs, then scoot off to catechism to learn about sin. Later I would change the bed sheets in the men's rooms. After that it was time to take a warm bath and submit to Elizabet's ministrations. In our family, this pattern of el sábado as a special day remained for many, many years.

A Faded Photograph

by Willie Morris

I CAME across a photograph of him not long ago, his black face with the long snout sniffing at something in the air, his tail straight and pointing, his eyes flashing in some momentary excitement. Looking at a faded photograph taken more than forty years before, even as a grown man, I would admit I still missed him.

It was 1943. I was nine years old and in the third grade when I saw him for the very first time. I had known we were getting him. My father had ordered him from a dog breeder he had heard about in Springfield, Missouri. Daddy had picked him up at the Illinois Central train depot, and when I came home that day from school he had just put the wire portable kennel on our back porch. I opened the door to the box and looked inside. I saw a little puppy drinking water from a container attached to the bottom. He glanced up at me.

"Come here, boy," I said.

He walked on unsteady legs toward me. I was sitting on the floor of the porch when he came out. He jumped into my lap and began nuzzling my hand with his nose. When I leaned toward him, he gave me a moist lick on my chin. Then he hugged me.

I led him into the house and gave him some puppy food in a dish. Then I followed him as he gingerly explored every room in the house. That night he jumped into my bed and stared at me, as if he were looking me over. Then, perhaps because he missed his mother in Missouri, he went to sleep in my arms. I was an only child, and he now was an only dog.

This was the first of our many days and years together. We named him Skipper for the lively way he walked, but he was always just Skip to me.

We had had a whole string of dogs before. When I was a very little boy we had big bird dogs, and then two purebred English smooth-haired fox terriers like this one, and I got to know all about dogs, a most precocious expert—their funny or crazy moods, how they looked when they were hungry or sick, when they were ready to bite and when their growling meant nothing, what they might be trying to say when they moaned and made strange human noises deep in their throats.

None of those other dogs ever came up to this one. You could talk to him as well as you could to many human beings, and *much* better than you could to some. He would sit down and look you straight in the eye, a long, mesmerizing gaze, and when he understood what you were saying he would turn his head sideways, back and forth, oscillating his whole body like the pendulum on a clock. Before going to sleep at night, with him sitting next to my face on the bed as he always did in such hours, I would say, "First thing tomorrow I want you to get your leash and then come get me up, because we're gonna get in the car and go out to the woods and get some *squirrels*," and the next morning sure enough he would get his leash, wake up both my father and me, walk nervously around the house with the leash in his mouth while we ate breakfast, and then lead us out to the car. Or I could say, "How about a little *swim?*" and his face would light up and he would push open the back door with his paws and escort me the quarter of a mile down the back alleyway to the swimming hole under the cypress near the bayou. Or, "Bubba's comin' over here today, and we're gonna play some *football*," and he would listen closely to this, and go out and wait around in front of the house and pick up Bubba's scent a block down the street and come tell me he was on his way. Or, "Skip, how about some *catch?*" and he would get up and walk into the front room, open a door in the antique cabinet with his improbable nose, and bring me his tennis ball.

I watched him grow up from the puppy who came to us from Missouri to the sleek, dexterous, affectionate creature who could do all these things, and more. He knew my father by the name of Big Boss. My mother was Bossie, and I was Little Boss or, interchangeably, Willie. (I called *him*, depending on the mood, Skip, Old Skip, and Boy. I have learned that when you love somebody, you will address him or her by different names.) Sometimes my father would hide in a closet and I would ask, "Skip, where's Big Boss?" and he would search the whole house, looking on every bed and under every chair and table until he arrived at the right closet, and began scratching it with his paws.

The town where Old Skip and I grew up together was an unhurried and isolated place then. About ten thousand people lived there, of all races and origins, and it sat there crazily, half on steep hills and half on the flat Delta. Some of the streets were not paved, and the main street, stretching its several blocks from the Dixie Theater down to the bend in the river, was narrow and plain, but down along the quiet, shady streets, with their magnolia and pecan and elm and locust trees, were the stately old houses that had been built long before the Civil War, slightly dark and decaying until the descendants became prosperous enough to have them "restored," which usually meant one coat of white enamel.

All this was before the big supermarkets and shopping centers and affluent subdivisions with no sidewalks and the monster highways and the innocence lost. It was even before there was television, and people would not close their doors and shut their curtains to watch the quiz games or the comedy hours or the talk shows where everybody talks at once. We would sit out on our front porches in the hot, serene nights and say hello to everyone who walked by. If the fire truck came past, we all got in our cars to follow it, and Skip was always the first to want to go. The houses were set out in a line under the soft green trees, their leaves rustling gently with the breeze. From the river sometimes came the melancholy echo of a boat's horn.

I knew the place then better than I did my own heart—every bend in every road, every house and every field, the exact spot where the robin went for her first crocus. It was not in my soul then, only in my pores, as familiar to me as rain or grass or sunlight. The town was poor one year and rich the next; everything in it pertained to cotton, and hence to usury and mortgage, debenture and labor. We lived and died by nature and followed the whims of the timeless clouds. Our people played seven-card stud against God.

It was a sly and silent town then, and Skip and my friends and I absorbed its every rhythm and heartbeat and the slightest sounds from far away. I loved those funny silences. The whole town was also abundant with alleys behind the paved thoroughfares inherited from an earlier day, little vagrant pathways running with scant design or reason behind the houses and stores and barns and chicken yards and gardens. You could get away with anything in those alleys. How Skip adored the freedom of them!

It was a lazy town, all stretched out on its hills and its flat streets, and over the years Skip also grew to know almost every house, tree, street, and alley. Occasionally he wandered around the town by himself, and everybody of any consequence knew who he was. Unbelievable as this may seem, Skip had the most curious and spooky way of sensing—don't ask me how—where I might be at any given moment, what a later day called ESP.

Our neighborhood was on one of the broad thoroughfares. In our side yard was a row of immense pecan trees shaped at the top like witches' caps, and in the back a huge field, vined and bosky. On the front lawn was a full, towering oak, one of Skip's favorite trees in the entire town.

Every time I shouted *"Squirrel!"* Skip would charge on the oak tree and try to climb it, sometimes getting as high as five or six feet with his spectacular leaps. This would stop traffic on the street in front of the house. People in cars would see him trying to shinny up the tree and would pull up to the curb and watch. They would signal to other passersby and point toward Skip, and these people would pull over too. They would gaze up into the tree to see what he was looking for, and, after a respectable pause, ask me, "What's he got up there?" and I would say, "Somethin' small and mean." They seldom recognized that Skip was just practicing.

This exercise was nothing to compare with football games, however. I cut the lace on a football and taught Old Skip how to carry it in his mouth, and how to hold it so he could avoid fumbles when he was tackled. I instructed him how to move on a quarterback's signals, to take a snap from center on the first bounce, and to follow me down the field. Ten or twelve of my comrades and I would organize a game of tackle in my front yard. Our side would go into a huddle, Skip included, and we would put our arms around one another's shoulders the way they did in real huddles at Ole Miss or Tennessee, and the dog would stand up on his hind legs and, with me kneeling, drape a leg around *my* shoulder. Then I would say, "Skip, pattern thirty-nine, off on three"; we would break out of the huddle with Skip dropping into the tailback position as I had taught him. Mutton-head or Peewee or Henjie or Bubba or Big Boy or Ralph would be the center, and I would station myself at quarterback and say, "Ready, set, one . . . two . . . *three*"; then the center would snap the ball on a hop to Skip, who would get it by the lace and follow me downfield, dodging would-be tacklers with no effort at all, weaving behind his blockers, spinning loose when he was cornered, sometimes balancing just inside the sidelines until he made it into the end zone. We would slap him on the back and say, nonchalantly, "Good run, boy," or when we had an audience: "Did you see my block back there?" Occasionally he would get tackled, but he seldom lost his grip on the ball, and he would always get up from the bottom of the pile and head straight for the huddle. He was an ideal safety man when the other side punted, and would get a grip on the second or third hop and gallop the length of the field for a touchdown. After considerable practice, I succeeded in teaching him the "Statue of Liberty" play, always shouting *"Statue of Liberty"* to him and our teammates before the play unfolded. I would take the snap from center and fade back in a low crouch, less a crouch than a forty-five-degree list, holding the ball behind my shoulder as if I were about to pass, all the while making sure the loosened lace was at a convenient angle. Skip, stationed at the left-end position, would circle around behind me, taking the lace of the pigskin between his teeth, then moving with deft assurance toward the right side of the line of scrimmage, where I was leading interference, whereupon he would follow his usual phalanx of blockers to the enemy's end zone for another spectacular score. *"Look at that dog playin' football!"* someone passing by would shout, and before the game was over we would have an incredulous crowd watching from cars or sitting on the sidelines, just as they did when he was after squirrels. The older men especially enjoyed this stunning spectacle. Walking down the sidewalk in front of the house, they would stop and let go with great whoops of astonishment: "Man, that's *some* dog. Can he catch a pass?"

For simple gratification, however, I believe Skip enjoyed our most imaginative intrigue above any other, and there are people still living in the town who will testify to it.

In that place and time, we began driving our parents' cars when we were thirteen years old; this was common practice then, and the town was so small that the policemen knew who you were, and your family, although they of course expected you to be careful. When I started driving our old four-door green DeSoto, I always took Skip on my trips around town. He rode with his snout extended far out the window, and if he caught the scent of one of the boys we knew, he would bark and point toward him, and we would stop and give that person a free ride. Skip would shake hands with our mutual friend, and lick him on the face and sit on the front seat between us. Cruising through the fringes of town, I would spot a group of old men standing around up the road. I would get Skip to prop himself against the steering wheel, his black head peering out of the windshield, while I crouched out of sight under the dashboard. Slowing the car to ten or fifteen, I would guide the steering wheel with my right hand while Skip, with his paws, kept it steady. As we drove by the Blue Front Café, I could hear one of the men shout: *"Look at that ol' dog drivin' a car!"*

Later we would ride out into the countryside, past the cotton fields and pecan groves and winding little creeks on the dark flat land toward some somnolent hamlet consisting of three or four unpainted stores, a minuscule wooden post office with its porch stacked with firewood in the wintertime, and a little graveyard nearby. Here the old men in overalls would be sitting on the gallery of the general store with patent-medicine posters on its sides, whittling wood or dipping snuff or swatting flies. When we slowly came past with Skip behind the steering wheel I heard one of them yell, *"A dog! A dog drivin'!"* and when I glanced slightly above the dashboard I sighted him falling out of his chair over the side of the porch into a privet hedge. One afternoon not long after that Henjie and Skip and I were out and about in the same country vicinity when far up the gravel road we saw a substantial congregation of humanity emerging from a backwoods church after a revival meeting. A number of the people, in fact, were still shouting and wailing as they approached their dusty parked cars and pickup trucks. I stopped the car and placed Skip at his familiar spot behind the steering wheel; then we slowly continued up the road. As we passed the church, in the midst of the avid cacophony a woman exclaimed: *"Is that a dog drivin' that car?"* The ensuing silence as we progressed on by was most horrendously swift and pervasive, and that sudden bucolic hush and quell remained unforgettable for me, as if the very spectacle of Old Skip driving that green DeSoto were inscrutable, celestial, and preordained.

Separate But Equal?

by Rose Blue and Corinne Naden

BARBARA JORDAN

Known for her powerful oratory skills, Barbara Jordan came from an impoverished background and rose to an outstanding career in law and government. She served from 1967-1973 as a Texas state senator, the first black woman elected in that capacity. From 1973-1979 she served in the U.S. House of Representatives, the first black congresswoman from the South. When she retired from public life, she became a professor. Ms. Jordan was the keynote speaker at the 1976 and 1992 Democratic National Conventions and was awarded the Presidential Medal of Freedom in 1994. Ms. Jordan lived for many years with multiple sclerosis and died of leukemia complications in 1996. Often quoted, one of her most famous sayings is, "What the people want is simple. They want an America as good as its promise." (Harvard University Commencement Address, June 16, 1977.)

BARBARA CHARLINE JORDAN was born on February 21, 1936, in Houston, Texas. The third child of Arlyne Jordan and her husband, Benjamin. Barbara had two older sisters, Rose Mary and Bennie.

The Jordan girls spent their early years in a pink-trimmed brick home in the Fifth Ward, one of the few black districts in Houston that boasted tall trees, paved streets, electricity, and residences with indoor plumbing. Sharing the two-bedroom house with the five Jordans were Benjamin Jordan's father, Charles, a truck driver and church deacon, and Charles's second wife, Alice, a high school English teacher. The parents and grandparents had their own rooms; the girls shared a fold-out bed in the dining room.

Closer to young Barbara than these relatives was her mother's father, John Ed Patten. A fiercely independent man who operated a junkyard, he adored his youngest granddaughter. She spent every Sunday with him, helping to sort the rags, scrap metal, and old newspapers that he collected and sold. "My grandfather always gave me part of the money," she recalled later. "We got on famously."

Grandfather Patten was the only man in Barbara's family who did not attend church. He often read to her from the Bible, however, and he decorated his property with such messages as The Lord Is My Shepherd and The Day of Wrath Is Come. He also gave his favorite granddaughter copious advice, much of which related to independence. "You just trot your own horse and don't get into the same rut as everyone else," he told her.

Patten had a favorite maxim, which Barbara memorized and which she quoted in her 1979 autobiography, *Barbara Jordan: A Self-Portrait:* "Just remember the world is not a playground, but a schoolroom. Life is not a holiday but an education. One eternal lesson for us all: to teach us how better we should love." That, said the adult Jordan, "was a very nice sentiment."

John Ed Patten had known more than his share of trouble: Crooked suppliers had swindled him out of a candy store he had once owned, and years before Barbara's birth he had served seven years in jail for shooting at—but not hitting—a white police officer he had mistaken for a thief. Despite his problems, the old man seemed serene and happy to Barbara. "Look, this man can make it, my grandfather," she said to herself. "He can put together whatever combination of things necessary and just kind of make it." Thinking about it years later, she said, "And that had an impact on me."

Patten had nurtured high hopes for his daughter Arlyne, Barbara's mother. As a young woman, Arlyne earned widespread praise as an orator at local Baptist conventions. "She was the most eloquent, articulate person I ever heard; if she'd been a man she would have been a preacher," recalled one impressed churchgoer. Arlyne's proud father encouraged her, helping her expand her vocabulary and acting as her speech coach.

Then, barely out of high school, Arlyne met and married Ben Jordan, a handsome student at Alabama's Tuskegee Institute, the college founded by prominent black leader Booker T. Washington in 1881. Arlyne's father was furious. He refused to attend her wedding and, as he watched her wait on her husband and spend her days cooking and cleaning, grew increasingly estranged.

But when Barbara (delivered by her mother's cousin, Dr. Thelma Patten) was born, John Patten felt a new surge of hope and love. He even began carrying a photograph of the baby, inscribed My Heart. "Here at last was someone to whom he could give all the lessons he had learned," wrote the adult Barbara. "He gave her a God who did not say bend your knee and await a better day. He gave her autonomy, telling her, 'Do not take a boss. Do not marry. Look at your mother.'" John Patten's grand-daughter never forgot his words.

All the Jordans were devout Baptists. Like her sisters, Barbara began attending church services before she could walk or talk; by the time she was 10, she had decided she was "tired of being a sinner" and joined the church as a full-fledged member. Ben Jordan watched with pride as his little girl "took the right hand of fellowship" in the Good Hope Missionary Baptist Church. Two years later, in 1947, he rose to his feet in the same church and announced that he had been "called to preach."

In 1949, when Barbara was 13, her father took on the full-time work of a minister in addition to his job at the Houston Terminal Warehouse and Cold Storage Company. At the same time, he moved his family out of his father's house and into their own home on Campbell Street. The new place was in one of Houston's poorest black neighborhoods, but the Jordans took great pride in it: Their neat wooden house was always crisply painted (in pink, the family's favorite color); its yard, trimly mowed. Ben Jordan set high standards both for himself and his family.

Jordan was a stern, exacting father. "He never struck us," recalled his oldest daughter, Rose Mary, "but the way he talked to us when he was displeased was more of a punishment than Mother's spankings. Just to have him question you frightened you to the point of never doing it again." The Jordan girls were allowed what Rose Mary called "limited recreational activities"; they were permitted to play with the other neighborhood children on summer evenings, she said, but only "till we were called in at curfew."

The Jordans taught their daughters to carry themselves with dignity, to value education and hard work, and to respect their elders. Barbara Jordan, who has been credited with exceptional self-control, has said she owes it to her father. She was absolutely forbidden to argue with him, no matter what the circumstances, a situation that taught her to keep her words and emotions in check.

The Jordan girls felt cherished and secure, but they lived under extremely tight discipline. Religion came first, and in the Jordan home that meant all-day services on Sunday, no dancing, no comic books or novels. The Jordans strongly encouraged their children to read, but only such approved material as the Bible or schoolbooks. "Our parents helped us with homework," Rose Mary has said, "especially Dad. He played a major role there."

Benjamin Jordan measured Rose Mary by his toughest standards. He expected her to be home from her dates exactly on time, to excel in school, and, because he had, to go to college. Tall, thin, and striking, she resembled her father in manner and looks. Bennie and Barbara, pretty girls who were sometimes mistaken for twins, were tall, too, but more rounded in build.

All the daughters were close to their mother, who was not quite as strict as her husband. Once, secretly defying household rules, she allowed an older cousin to take the girls to a Shirley Temple movie. That was a red-letter day, the subject of hours of whispered conversations and smothered giggles. Even as adults, Barbara and her sisters kept a special place in their hearts for the dimpled, curly-haired star who sang "On the Good Ship Lollypop."

Benjamin Jordan would no doubt have frowned on that song, but he loved music and made it an important element in his family's life. He and his wife, both accomplished musicians, played the piano and sang well—mostly, of course, Baptist hymns. Insisting that all three girls take piano lessons, the Jordans engaged a dedicated but tough teacher, Miss Mattie Thomas.

Thomas took no nonsense, demanding that her students practice every day and that they give yearly public recitals. Barbara was fond of music and enjoyed playing the guitar, but she hated the piano lessons and the performances. She submitted to Thomas's regimen for two years, then revolted. No more grueling hours of practice, she told Thomas, and no more miserable recitals. The astonished teacher rushed to Barbara's father; his daughter, she snorted, had treated her in a most "highhanded way."

Ben Jordan reacted to Thomas's complaint with predictable outrage. Not only had his youngest daughter shown disrespect to her elders; she had dared to disobey him! A family storm broke, but in the end, Barbara stood her ground. She and her father, both of them strong-willed and stubborn, would have many such clashes during her childhood years and beyond.

The two of them, in fact, "did not see eye to eye on anything," said Barbara Jordan. She recalled an occasion when she heard him talking to a friend about his daughters: "They don't drink, they don't smoke, they don't dance, they don't play cards, they don't go to the movies," said Preacher Jordan. His words, said his rebellious youngest child, "caused me the squeemies of the gut. I thought: 'How can he go around bragging about the fact that he has three freaks?'"

Next to his children's morality, nothing concerned Benjamin Jordan more than their education. "No man can take away your brain," he often told the girls. He wanted them to study, to think clearly, and to speak well. In love with language, he insisted that they pronounce English with precision and speak it with power and conviction. Here, Barbara did not disappoint him.

As she grew up, she actually overtook her father in zeal. If she got one B out of a row of A's on her report card, he was puzzled, but she was outraged. Nothing less than a straight-A average would satisfy her.

"Barbara always had a mind of her own," recalled Rose Mary. "She was the driving force in the family." Armed with the values, discipline, and respect for hard work she learned from her father, Barbara developed her own strict code of principles. Her attitudes were further honed by the era of pervasive racial discrimination in which she grew up.

Most young Americans of today, black and white, know racism and segregation ruled the land before the civil rights movement of the mid-1950s and the 1960s. They may, however, find it hard to understand the degree to which racial discrimination affected the life of all Americans. Throughout Barbara Jordan's formative years, her skin color made her, in effect, a second-class citizen.

Discrimination found its way into every part of American life, in schools and restaurants and buses, in playgrounds and movie theaters, at beaches and ball games, in neighborhoods and apartment houses. If you were black, particularly in the South, you lived in segregated housing and sent your children to segregated schools. You rode in the back of the bus, and if a white person was standing, you gave up your seat. You used "colored" water fountains and rest rooms.

If you found yourself in a strange neighborhood or unfamiliar town, you might have trouble finding a place that would serve you food or rent you a room. You would, of course, try not to find yourself in an unfamiliar neighborhood. In places where white people made the rules, potential trouble always lurked. It might take the form of hostile stares or taunts from passing whites; it might be worse if a band of white supremacists—the Ku Klux Klan, for example—happened to be roaming around looking for "uppity blacks." A confrontation with these hooded terrorists could result in a beating or even in murder.

In Houston, as in other cities across the land, blacks freely entered "white territory" to work, perhaps as chauffeurs or nursemaids, but at the end of the day they left quickly. Their own segregated neighborhoods might be poor and shabby, but they were relatively free of suspicious white policemen eager to pick them up on any pretext at all.

Under these circumstances, most black parents understand-ably tried to keep their children close to home for as long as possible. As a result, the youngsters often grew up with only a vague concept of the larger world. Barbara Jordan said that in her childhood, everyone she knew was poor and black, as she was herself. "Since I didn't see movies, and we didn't have tele-vision, and I didn't go anyplace with anybody else," she wrote in her autobiography, "how could I know anything else to con-sider?" For Barbara, the community of white people might as well have been on another planet.

The Jordan girls remained in their own segregated world far past childhood. When Rose Mary graduated from high school in 1949, she headed for Prairie View College, a nearby all-black in-stitution. That same year, Barbara joined her other sister, Bennie, at Houston's all-black Phillis Wheatley High School. (The school was named for an African-born woman who had arrived in Boston as a slave in 1753. Freed by her master when she was in her twenties, Wheatley had gone on to become the first published black American poet.)

Far brighter than average, Barbara enjoyed school. She es-tablished a strong-knit "gang," wore fashionable toeless shoes, had a smooth pageboy haircut, and rooted wildly for the school football team. ("I wasn't a cheerleader," she recalled, "but I should have been.") She disliked physical education—"I didn't want to put on the gym shorts," she said—but she did well in all her other classes and in her many extracurricular activities, es-pecially debating.

Barbara's effectiveness as a debater came from more than the strong, resonant voice she inherited from her mother. Schooled by her father and grandfather, she demonstrated an unusually keen ability to marshal and articulate her arguments, enabling her to overwhelm debating opponents with a one-two punch: drama backed by logic.

Barbara entered—and frequently won—scores of formal de-bates, some of them with Wheatley students, some with teams from other local schools. Her high ratings propelled her to the 1952 Ushers Oratorical Contest, a Baptist-sponsored event held in Waco, Texas. Competing with star black speech-makers from high schools all over the state, Barbara won first prize: $50 and an expense-paid trip to the national contest in Chicago.

Escorted by her mother, the young woman from Campbell Street took a train to the Illinois city. Here, at the Greater

Bethesda Baptist Church, she would do her best to outshine dozens of other contestants, all of them male. Wearing a long pink evening dress, Barbara took the stage to deliver an impassioned oration about "The Necessity for a Higher Education."

"Today's youth are living in a confused world," asserted the teenager. Then, addressing an imaginary opponent who would deny college admittance to qualified candidates, she rolled into high gear. "You are not only refusing to one out of two of the youth in this country the opportunity to do the work for which they have been preparing themselves," she said with conviction, "but you are also deliberately refusing to give them the intellectual and moral guidance they need and that the world of tomorrow is to need." Commenting on her speech afterward, Barbara said, "the main thing I was saying was: 'Folks, a higher education is on the way in. It's the only way out of the fix you're in.'"

Barbara was rather pleased with her oration, and she had a right to be. The *Houston Informer* for July 17, 1952, carried this story: "Miss Barbara Charline Jordan, daughter of the Reverend and Mrs. Benjamin M. Jordan of 4910 Campbell Street, added to her long list of oratorical awards [at] the National United Ushers Association of America. . . . Miss Jordan represented the state of Texas and . . . won first place, [receiving] a $200 scholarship to the school of her choice and a literary medal."

The *Informer,* which went on to note that "the talented young woman won praise and congratulations from educational circles all over the state," added that Barbara "had the distinction of having been chosen 'Girl of the Year' [at Wheatley], and is winner of the Julius Levy Oratorical Contest award. . . . She also holds three district and two state championship medals in Junior and Senior declamation, respectively, and a medal for outstanding accomplishments in speech."

Concluding its story, the newspaper quoted Barbara Jordan's comment on winning the national contest. "It's just another milestone I have passed," she said. "It's just the beginning."

from

Full Circle

by Dan Jansen with Jack McCallum

DAN JANSEN
The youngest of nine children, Dan Jansen was born into a family that loved speed skating. He started the sport when he was four years old. An all-around athlete, he broke several world records. He was seen as somewhat of a tragic figure due to his inability to win Olympic medals for many years and the loss of his sister from leukemia. Finally, in 1994, he won the gold medal and established a new world record for the 1000-meter race. He is currently working as a sports commentator, having retired from competition.

MAYBE I never would've started skating if Mary, the oldest, hadn't been prone to sickness in the winter months. Mary was a terrific athlete but didn't have many opportunities to participate in sports once it got cold, so she tended to lie around the house and cough a lot. My father thought it was because she was inside all the time. So one Sunday morning he decided to take her over to McCarty Park, which is only a quarter mile from our house, to watch the North American Skating Championships. Mary was about ten years old and had never had a pair of skates on her feet. As she watched the competitors, she turned to my dad and said, "I can do that."

And that's how the Jansen family started skating.

It was fortunate that Mary went out that day, but it wasn't necessarily preordained. Had she not started and been successful, maybe I would've paid more attention to football and baseball. Who knows? It's entirely possible. But once it happened, West Allis was an ideal place to develop as a speed skater, maybe *the* best place in the country. The West Allis Speed Skating Club was born during the Depression in the 1930s and is still going strong today. In most other Wisconsin towns boys start playing hockey automatically, but in West Allis they begin speed-skating. The tradition was there. As early as 1936 a guy named Del Lamb from the club made the Olympics, and in 1956 William Carow did it with Lamb as his coach. One of the most famous West Allis guys to make the Olympics was Wayne LeBombard, in 1964 and '68. And then came a few guys I knew—Mike Woods and Tom and Mike Plant.

Mary had a knack for skating right away and became a state champion. The skating back then, the kind we all started in, was pack-style, the kind you see in Olympic short-track skating. Janet used to go watch Mary from the warming house, and gradually she took it up, and then so did Diane. Janet became a state champ, too, and was actually the first Jansen to skate the 500 meters on an official oval. She went under 48 seconds the first time she tried it, and my mother remembers that everyone was talking about it. (As a basis for comparison, Bonnie Blair now skates it under 40 seconds.) But none of my sisters had any professional training, and, had they been born later, in an era when girls were "supposed" to be athletes, I think they could've gone far, maybe even been world-class. But for them it was largely a social event. Jane always said that her favorite memory of youth skating was watching Eric Heiden, who was from Madison but who used to come over and skate in West Allis, take off his pants to change into his skating tights right in the middle of the rink. That activity was eventually banned. Janet remembers being shocked one day when Mrs. LeBombard, who was involved in youth skating, said to her, "With the right training, we're gonna have two inches on those thighs by the end of the summer." That is not what Janet wanted to hear.

Our parents never, ever pushed us into skating. That's important to remember. Diane tried it, had some success, but didn't really pursue it. That was fine. Joanne tried it, wasn't very successful at all, and asked Dad if she could quit. He was genuinely perplexed by the question. "Why would you do something you don't like?" he said. So Joanne hung up the skates.

After Mary and Janet set the pace, my brothers just naturally followed. Jim was an above-average skater but could never beat the real good guys who were around then, one of them being Pete Mueller, who later became my coach. Dick, however, was really good, and in many ways he's the most remarkable skater of any of us. I wasn't born when this happened, but my father remembers Dick at a meet when he was about five years old wearing a pair of white girls' figure skates laced up around his ankles. He took off in this race, but they fired the gun a second time to indicate a restart. Dick either didn't hear the gun or didn't care. He kept on going all the way around the track, never noticing that everyone else was back at the starting line. When he finished, he just wouldn't believe that he hadn't won the race, and he refused to go back to the line. There's a stubborn kid.

Dick won several state championships and finished third in the nationals as a junior but concentrated on other sports in high school, like football, swimming, and track. He decided to get back into skating a few years ago, and since then he's won consecutive national championships in the masters' division, which is for skaters thirty-five to fifty years of age. He also had a goal of trying to qualify for the Olympic trials in 1992, which took an unbelievable commitment on his part. He's a sergeant in the West Allis police department and works the midnight–to–8 A.M. shift. He'd change into his skating clothes at work, go directly to a workout, come home, shower, grab something to eat, lie down for a couple hours, do an afternoon workout, then go directly to work again. Unbelievable.

The cutoff time to make the trials was 40.5 seconds for the 500 meters, and Dick made it on his last attempt. (I'm not the only Jansen with a sense of drama.) So in 1992, Dick, Mike, and I were all in the trials, the first time in history that three members of the same family competed. Unbelievably, Dick, at the age of thirty-six, skated well enough to make the trials again in 1994. He is a remarkable, remarkable athlete. He was also Mike's and my first coach, the first guy to really show us about gliding instead of just running on skates.

In a way, then, it was easiest for Mike and me. There was a standard of excellence already set, a Jansen skating tradition, by the time we started. There was also a nice, new outdoor rink in West Allis. So Mike and I could only roll our eyes when Dick would tell us about walking a mile in a snowstorm, shoveling off a pond, and then getting kicked off by the police when you were all done. I'm sure I'll have to invent something to tell Janie about how tough I had it, too.

My first pair of skates were double-runners, and my first real pair were hand-me-downs, probably from Dick. I was only four or five years old when I skated in my first pack-style meets. I'm told that both Mike and I preferred throwing snowballs and rolling down hills to actually competing, and the meet organizers used to bribe us with nickels and candy bars just to get us to the starting line. I was pretty successful from the beginning, though rarely the best. That honor belonged to Mike, who is about eighteen months older than I am. Most of the time we competed in different divisions, but he dominated his, whereas I was more like a second- or third-place skater. In the West Allis

Speed Skating Club program the national outdoor pack-style champions from the club are listed. I'm mentioned once. Mike is in there four times.

There's a speed-skating circuit around Wisconsin, Minnesota, and Illinois, and from an early age Mike and I, just like Mary, Janet, and Dick before us, jumped right into it. At one time or another, my parents' entire weekend life was devoted to loading up the Volkswagen van, making sandwiches, packing sweaters, tying skates, and drying tears of disappointment. I don't know how they did it. By the time Mike and I really got into it, Mary and Janet were out of it, of course, but there was rarely a time when there weren't at least three Jansen kids competing.

How about this for a schedule? My father would come home on Friday night after working his four-to-midnight shift at the West Allis police department, and begin sharpening skates, sometimes three pairs, sometimes five. It would take him almost two hours. Meanwhile, my mother would be making peanut-butter-and-jelly sandwiches. Then they'd go to bed, maybe about 2:30, wake up at 5:30, and drive us all to Madison or Minneapolis or Chicago. Much of that time my father held another part-time job, too, driving a truck or landscaping or something like that. And my mom went back to work as a nurse from time to time. But they always had enough time to cart us around. Always. It was a way of life. And if the meet was on Sunday, you could add in a stop at church, too.

People always talked about how hard it must've been for my parents to watch me fail in the Olympics in '88 and '92. But hard didn't begin in 1988. Hard was putting on five layers of clothing to start the car at 5 A.M. for a four-hour drive. Hard was watching me stumble and fall and cry when I was ten years old. For my sisters, hard was convincing their boyfriends and husbands that where they wanted to be on a Sunday morning was watching some snot-nosed kid skate around a frozen pond. But that was just part of Jansen family life. If someone was doing something, the rest of the family was there. And it wasn't just sports—my sisters still remember getting up at 5 A.M. to watch Jim be an altar boy for the first time. Gee, sorry I missed that.

One memory from those early days sticks out. It was in 1977, when I was eleven years old and the national championship meet was in Minnesota. Mike won his division, his first national title, and I was in a good position to win mine. But coming around a turn in one of the races, I tripped on a rubber hose they had set up as a lane marker. (No jokes, please.) That slip cost me the national title by one point.

I started crying. I kept crying as my mom took off my skates, and I kept crying throughout the award ceremonies, and I kept crying when we got into the car, and I was still crying when we pulled into our driveway back in West Allis six hours later. I don't know why Mike, who shared the backseat with me, didn't kill me.

As we got out of the car, my father, who hadn't spoken a word to me all the way home, turned around and said, very quietly, "You know, Dan, there's more to life than skating in a circle."

Later in life, I came to truly know the importance of those words.

I don't think there's one prescribed way you become a champion. Pete Mueller, for example, who won a gold medal in the 1,000 in the 1976 Olympics, was a guy who did it largely on his own. He was an independent type who didn't need much support from his family and friends. But if I know anything, I know that having a large and supportive family in my corner has been the single most important plus in my career. Who knows why? But there have been times, maybe when I've been trailing in a race or faltering in my training, when I've literally been able to feel their strength and their collective will pushing me onward. I don't know whether I've ever thanked them properly for that, so that's what I'm doing now.

"I Want Some Sentimental Effusions of the Heart"

by Natalie S. Bober

ABIGAIL ADAMS
Wife of President John Adams, Abigail Adams is known for her extensive letters, written to her husband during the American Revolution. Her grandson, Charles, later collected and published these letters. While her husband was away in Philadelphia and, later, Europe, Abigail oversaw the daily business of the farm household and raised their five children. An independent person, Mrs. Adams was an early supporter of women's education. She died of typhoid at the age of 74.

THE First Continental Congress which had assembled in Carpenter's Hall in Philadelphia on September 5, 1774, had been summoned not for independence but for liberty as Americans understood that word. They were struggling to preserve the freedom the colonies already had. Independence was not a conscious goal. It was viewed as a last resort. Yet early in 1775, as her husband wrote a series of newspaper essays defending the rights of the colonies, Abigail wrote to Mercy, "We cannot be happy without being free, . . . we cannot be free without being secure in our property. . . . We know too well the blessings of freedom, to tamely resign it."

"Is it not better to die the last of British freemen than live the first of British Slaves?" she asked Mercy. When she read George III's speech at the opening of Parliament on November 20, published in the *Massachusetts Spy* on February 2, she continued her letter, "The die is cast. . . . Heaven only knows what is next to take place but it seems to me the Sword is now our only, yet dreadful alternative."

Then, just two and a half months later, on the clear, cold morning of Wednesday, April 19, 1775, the first shots of the American Revolution were fired at Lexington and Concord. The war with England had begun. The dreaded message, carried frantically by word of mouth and galloping express, moved across the land in shock waves.

Abigail's worst fears had become a reality. Yet now she felt calmer than she had in months. The crisis she had been certain was unavoidable had finally occurred, and she refused to panic. John's presence at home helped.

But just one week later Delegate Adams was on his way to Philadelphia again to join the Second Continental Congress. When he left home he was sick to his stomach, feverish, and numb with horror and foreboding. The other delegates had left without him two days before. Now Abigail saw him off in a horse-drawn cart borrowed from her father, with a young man to look after him, a cake from her mother, and pleas to take his medicine. She tried to be "heroick," but confessed that her "heart felt like a heart of Led."

Once again, Abigail and the children were alone, just half an hour's ride from the American lines encircling the British army in Boston. Boston had become, in effect, a British camp, closed off from the rest of New England. Many houses, including the Adamses' house on Queen Street, had been taken over by the British army. For the most part, the redcoats allowed no one to enter or leave the city. A short time later a few people were permitted to leave each day, but they could take with them very few of their possessions. These weary refugees from Boston, many with their little children in tow, needed a place to go. Abigail, as did many of her neighbors, housed as many people as she could—for "a day, a night, a week."

As Massachusetts was plunged into the fierce tumult of the American Revolution, every alarm sent minutemen marching past Abigail's front door, hungry, thirsty, looking for a place to rest. The indomitable Abigail tried to accommodate the soldiers also. One night she housed an entire company of militia on their way to join the encampments outside Boston. Some of the soldiers slept in the attic, some in the barn. A few spread blankets on the parlor floor. The next morning, as they drilled in the field behind the house, little Johnny proudly marched up and down with them.

"The house is a Scene of Confusion . . . you can hardly imagine how we live," Abigail wrote to John a month after he had left. Three weeks later, when she still had not heard from John, she was unable to conceal her distress. She wrote to her absent husband:

> I set down to write to you a monday, but really could not compose myself sufficiently: the anxiety I suffered from not hearing one syllable from you for more than five weeks; and the new distress ariseing from the arrival of recruits agitated me more than I have been. . . .

Perhaps, the very next Letter I write will inform you that I am driven away from our, yet quiet cottage. . . . Courage I know we have in abundance, conduct I hope we shall not want, but powder—where shall we get a sufficient supply?

. . . You tell me you know not when you shall see me. I never trust myself long with the terrors which sometimes intrude themselves upon me.

I hope we shall see each other again and rejoice together in happier Days. The little ones are well and send Duty to Pappa. Dont fail of letting me hear from you by every opportunity, every line is like a precious Relict of the Saints.

She continued with a practical request: would John purchase a "bundle of pins" for her? The "cry" of pins was "great." "Pray, don't . . . forget my pins," she reminded him the following month. "Not one pin to be had for love or money."

"We live in Continual Expectation of Hostilities. Scarcely a day that does not produce some," she told her husband. But she described herself as "very brave upon the whole," then went on to ask John how much Congress knew about the suffering of Boston: "Does every Member feel for us? Can they realize what we suffer? And can they believe with what patience and fortitude we endure the conflict?"

Much to his wife's dismay, John occasionally showed her letters to fellow delegates in the hope that they would understand. He told a friend, "There is a Lady at the Foot of Pens Hill, who obliges me with clearer and fuller Intelligence, than I can get from a whole Committee of Gentlemen."

Fearful that British redcoats might attack coastal towns like Braintree and Weymouth, John wrote to Abigail that if an attack actually came, she must "fly to the Woods with our Children. Give my tenderest love to them."

In fact, the conflict did come to Braintree, causing many to flee when the British raided nearby Grape Island to take off hay for their horses. Both of John's brothers were members of the militia and shouldered muskets in this and other frequent conflicts. But Abigail was not one to panic. She knew that should she be in real danger, she could accept her brother-in-law Peter's offer of the safety of his home, further inland and away from the scene of the fighting. But for now, she would wait and see.

When the first major battle came, Abigail chose to remain,

and even to be a witness. Before dawn on Saturday, June 17, she was awakened by the sound of far-off gunfire. All through the sweltering morning, as she went about her chores, the dull boom of cannon intruded on her consciousness.

Finally she took seven-year-old Johnny by the hand and together they walked to the top of Penn's Hill and climbed up on the rocks for a better view. In horror they stared across the blue bay and into the black, smoking mass that was all that was left of Charlestown. Her father's birthplace had been burned to the ground. John Quincy never forgot the scene.

Abigail and Johnny walked slowly back home, tears blurring their eyes. Soon riders on the Coast Road to Plymouth stopped at the farmhouse for a drink of water. They told of the great battle under way on Bunker Hill* in Charlestown. One brought word that the beloved Dr. Joseph Warren had been killed in the fighting.

Third only to Sam Adams and John Hancock as a political leader of the radical Whig party, Dr. Warren had gone into battle as a volunteer. He had insisted on fighting side by side with the soldiers, who were heartened by his courage. Hit on the right side of his head with a musket ball, he died instantly. Whispered accounts said he was beheaded. He had been a widower and the father of four young children.

It was Joseph Warren who, on April 18, had dispatched his good friend Paul Revere, a trusted express rider as well as Boston's most gifted silversmith, to warn Sam Adams and John Hancock that the British might make a sudden march to seize both them and the stores of powder in Concord.

Joseph Warren had been the Adamses' good friend and their family doctor in Boston. His skill in setting a "very bad fracture" had recently saved Johnny from the loss of a finger. Now he was dead at the age of thirty-four, his fine clothes soaked with blood. "Everybody remembered his fine, silk fringed waistcoat," a British officer later recalled.

Nabby and Johnny were bewildered and sad. Abigail was distraught. She gave vent to her feelings in a letter to John the next day: "The Day; perhaps the decisive Day is come on which the fate of America depends. My bursting Heart must find vent at my pen." She went on to tell him of Dr. Warren's death: he "fell gloriously fighting for his Country. . . . Great is our Loss."

Quoting from the Bible, she continued: "The race is not to the swift, nor the battle to the strong, but the God of Israel is he that giveth strength and power unto his people. Trust in him at all times. . . . God is a refuge for us." At times of stress Abigail turned to her faith in God to sustain her.

She continued her letter: "Charlestown is laid in ashes. The Battle began upon our intrenchments upon Bunker Hill, a Saturday morning about 3 o'clock and has not ceased yet and tis now 3 o'clock Sabbath afternoon." She ended by telling her husband: "I cannot compose myself to write any further at present."

Two days later Abigail concluded her letter, alluding once again to the death of Dr. Warren: "The tears of multitudes pay tribute to his memory."

John responded by telling his wife, "You are really brave, my dear, you are an Heroine."

And she continued to be a heroine. One day Johnny came into the house to find his mother and his uncle Elihu, dressed in his minuteman uniform, a hunting shirt with a musket slung on his back. The two were in the kitchen, putting all his mother's treasured pewter spoons into a large kettle. As Johnny watched his mother calmly directing the activity in her quiet voice, he slowly began to understand that they were melting down her precious pewter to make bullets. As his eyes met hers across the room, he felt a surge of love and pride.

"Do you wonder," said John Quincy Adams sixty-eight years later, "that a boy of seven who witnessed this scene should be a patriot?"

By July 1775 every bed in Braintree was filled by families forced to flee from occupied Boston. Abigail reorganized her household to accommodate an entire family in which there was an expectant mother.

"It would make your heart ake to see what difficulties and distresses the poor Boston people are driven to," she wrote to John.

As she continued to help the displaced people, supervise the mowing of the hay, keep the caterpillars out of the fruit trees, worry that the drought they were experiencing that summer might damage the crops, and, of course, care for her "little brood," she still found time to write. But she playfully complained, "I have received a good deal of paper from you; I wish it had been more covered." She reproached John for his short letters, yet she acknowledged, "I must not grumble. I know your time is not yours, nor mine."

As if to compensate, her letters to him grew longer, filled with details of the war in Massachusetts, and of their family and domestic concerns. She was pleased when John called her his

*Bunker Hill: It was actually Breed's Hill.

"home-front reporter," telling her that her letters "contain more particulars than any Letters I had before received from any Body."

More than ever now, letter writing became a way of life for her. "There are perticular times when I feel such an uneasiness, such a restlessness, as neither Company, Books, family Cares or any other thing will remove, my Pen is my only pleasure." As she committed her thoughts to paper, she gained a clearer understanding of her own role as a wife and mother. Her letters became, in effect, a revealing source of self-analysis. They frequently varied in information and opinions, but never in their tenderness and thoughtfulness. She might be emotionally upset, but she was always conscious of her husband's enormous responsibility. And she was always intellectually keen, turning to examples from history to help her understand what was happening around her.

She seemed to feel that as a woman she could best show her patriotism by supporting her husband in his work for their country. She understood that John was genuinely torn between his public and private life, and that he suffered when he was forced to be away from his family for long periods of time. She didn't ask him to choose between them.

But there were times when she felt overwhelmed by all her responsibilities: "I want you for my protector," she pleaded. A few days later she couldn't resist chiding him:

> All the letters I receive from you seem to be wrote in so much haste, that they scarcely leave room for a social feeling. They let me know that you exist, but some of them contain scarcely six lines. I want some sentimental Effusions of the Heart. . . . I lay claim to a Larger Share than I have had.

She ended that letter:

> Our little ones send Duty to Pappa. You would smile to see them all gather round mamma upon the reception of a letter to hear from pappa, and Charles with open mouth, What does par say—did not he write no more. And little Tom says I wish I could see par.

She never lost her sense of humor. She told John that Charles, now five, asks, "Mar, who is for us and who against us?" John would laugh, she told him, to see the children run at the sight of his letters—"like chickens for a crumb, when the Hen clucks."

First Adventures

At Last I Kill a Buffalo

by Chief Luther Standing Bear

AT last the day came when my father allowed me to go on a buffalo hunt with him. And what a proud boy I was!

Ever since I could remember my father had been teaching me the things that I should know and preparing me to be a good hunter. I had learned to make bows and to string them; and to make arrows and tip them with feathers. I knew how to ride my pony no matter how fast he would go, and I felt that I was brave and did not fear danger. All these things I had learned for just this day when father would allow me to go with him on a buffalo hunt. It was the event for which every Sioux boy eagerly waited. To ride side by side with the best hunters of the tribe, to hear the terrible noise of the great herds as they ran, and then to help to bring home the kill was the most thrilling day of any Indian boy's life. The only other event which could equal it would be the day I went for the first time on the warpath to meet the enemy and protect my tribe.

On the following early morning we were to start, so the evening was spent in preparation. Although the tipis were full of activity, there was no noise nor confusion outside. Always the evening before a buffalo hunt and when every one was usually in his tipi, an old man went around the circle of tipis calling, "I-ni-la," "I-ni-la," not loudly, but so every one could hear. The old man was saying, "Keep quiet," "Keep quiet." We all knew that the scouts had come in and reported buffalo near and that we must all keep the camp in stillness. It was not necessary for the old man to go into each tipi and explain to the men that to-morrow there would be a big hunt, as the buffalo were coming. He did not order the men to prepare their weapons and neither did he order the mothers to keep children from crying. The one word, "I-ni-la," was sufficient to bring quiet to the whole camp. That night there would be no calling or shouting from tipi to tipi and no child would cry aloud. Even the horses and dogs obeyed the command for quiet, and all night not a horse neighed and not a dog barked. The very presence of quiet was everywhere. Such is the orderliness of a Sioux camp that men, women, children, and animals seem to have a common understanding and sympathy. It is no mystery but natural that the Indian and his animals understand each other very well both with words and without words. There are words, however, that the Indian uses that are understood by both his horses and dogs. When on a hunt, if one of the warriors speaks the word "A-a-ah" rather quickly and sharply, every man, horse, and dog will stop instantly and listen. Not a move will be made by an animal until the men move or speak further. As long as the hunters listen, the animals will listen also.

The night preceding a buffalo hunt was always an exciting night, even though it was quiet in camp. There would be much talk in the tipis around the fires. There would be sharpening of arrows and of knives. New bow-strings would be made and quivers would be filled with arrows.

It was in the fall of the year and the evenings were cool as father and I sat by the fire and talked over the hunt. I was only eight years of age, and I know that father did not expect me to get a buffalo at all, but only to try perhaps for a small calf should I be able to get close enough to one. Nevertheless, I was greatly excited as I sat and watched father working in his easy, firm way.

I was wearing my buffalo-skin robe, the hair next to my body. Mother had made me a rawhide belt and this, wrapped around my waist, held my blanket on when I threw it off my shoulders. In the early morning I would wear it, for it would be cold. When it came time to shoot, I should not want my blanket but the belt would hold it in place.

You can picture me, I think, as I sat in the glow of the campfire, my little brown body bare to the waist watching, and listening intently to my father. My hair hung down my back and I wore moccasins and breech-cloth of buckskin. To my belt was fastened a rawhide holster for my knife, for when I was eight years of age we had plenty of knives. I was proud to own a knife, and this night I remember I kept it on all night. Neither did I lay aside my bow, but went to sleep with it in my hand, thinking, I suppose, to be all the nearer ready in the morning when the start was made.

Father sharpened my steel points for me and also sharpened my knife. The whetstone was a long stone which was kept in a buckskin bag, and sometimes this stone went all over the camp; every tipi did not have one, so we shared this commodity with one another. I had as I remember about ten arrows, so when father was through sharpening them I put them in my rawhide quiver. I had a rawhide quirt, too, which I would wear fastened to my waist. As father worked, he knew I was watching him closely and listening whenever he spoke. By the time all preparations had been made, he had told me just how I was to act when I started out in the morning with the hunters.

We went to bed, my father hoping that tomorrow would be successful for him so that he could bring home some nice meat for the family and a hide for my mother to tan. I went to bed, but could not go to sleep at once, so filled was I with the wonderment and excitement of it all. The next day was to be a test for me. I was to prove to my father whether he was or was not justified in his pride in me. What would be the result of my training? Would I be brave if I faced danger and would father be proud of me? Though I did not know it that night I was to be tried for the strength of my manhood and my honesty in this hunt. Something happened that day which I remember above all things. It was a test of my real character and I am proud to say that I did not find myself weak, but made a decision that has been all these years a gratification to me.

The next morning the hunters were catching their horses about daybreak. I arose with my father and went out and caught my pony. I wanted to do whatever he did and show him that he did not have to tell me what to do. We brought our animals to the tipi and got our bows and arrows and mounted. From over the village came the hunters. Most of them were leading their running horses. These running horses were anxious for the hunt and came prancing, their ears straight up and their tails waving in the air. We were joined with perhaps a hundred or more riders, some of whom carried bows and arrows and some armed with guns.

The buffalo were reported to be about five or six miles away as we should count distance now. At that time we did not measure distance in miles. One camping distance was about ten miles, and these buffalo were said to be about one half camping distance away.

Some of the horses were to be left at a stopping-place just before the herd was reached. These horses were pack-animals which were taken along to carry extra blankets or weapons. They were trained to remain there until the hunters came for them. Though they were neither hobbled nor tied, they stood still during the shooting and noise of the chase.

My pony was a black one and a good runner. I felt very important as I rode along with the hunters and my father, the chief. I kept as close to him as I could.

Two men had been chosen to scout or to lead the party. These two men were in a sense policemen whose work it was to keep order. They carried large sticks of ash wood, something like a policeman's billy, though longer. They rode ahead of the party while the rest of us kept in a group close together. The leaders went ahead until they sighted the herd of grazing buffalo. Then they stopped and waited for the rest of us to ride up. We all rode slowly toward the herd, which on sight of us had come together, although they had been scattered here and there over the plain. When they saw us, they all ran close together as if at the command of a leader. We continued riding slowly toward the herd until one of the leaders shouted, "Ho-ka-he!" which means, "Ready, Go!" At that command every man started for the herd. I had been listening, too, and the minute the hunters started, I started also.

Away I went, my little pony putting all he had into the race. It was not long before I lost sight of father, but I kept going just the same. I threw my blanket back and the chill of the autumn morning struck my body, but I did not mind. On I went. It was wonderful to race over the ground with all these horsemen about me. There was no shouting, no noise of any kind except the pounding of the horses' feet. The herd was now running and had raised a cloud of dust. I felt no fear until we had entered this cloud of dust and I could see nothing about me—only hear the sound of feet. Where was father? Where was I going? On I rode through the cloud, for I knew I must keep going.

Then all at once I realized that I was in the midst of the buffalo, their dark bodies rushing all about me and their great heads moving up and down to the sound of their hoofs beating upon the earth. Then it was that fear overcame me and I leaned close down upon my little pony's body and clutched him tightly. I can never tell you how I felt toward my pony at that moment. All thought of shooting had left my mind. I was seized by blank fear. In a moment or so, however, my senses became clearer, and I could distinguish other sounds beside the clatter of feet. I could hear a shot now and then and I could see the buffalo beginning to break up into small bunches. I could not see father nor any of my companions yet, but my fear was vanishing and I was safe. I let my pony run. The buffalo looked too large for me to tackle, anyway, so I just kept going. The buffalo became more and more scattered. Pretty soon I saw a young calf that looked about my size. I remembered now what father had told me the night before as we sat about the fire. Those instructions were important for me now to follow.

I was still back of the calf, being unable to get alongside of him. I was anxious to get a shot, yet afraid to try, as I was still very nervous. While my pony was making all speed to come alongside, I chanced a shot and to my surprise my arrow landed. My second arrow glanced along the back of the animal and sped on between the horns, making only a slight wound. My third arrow hit a spot that made the running beast slow up in his gait. I shot a fourth arrow, and though it, too, landed it was not a fatal wound. It seemed to me that it was taking a lot of shots, and I was not proud of my marksmanship. I was glad, however, to see the animal going slower and I knew that one more shot would make me a hunter. My horse seemed to know his own importance. His two ears stood straight forward and it was not necessary for me to urge him to get closer to the buffalo. I was soon by the side of the buffalo and one more shot brought the chase to a close. I jumped from my pony, and as I stood by my fallen game, I looked all around wishing that the world could see. But I was alone. In my determination to stay by until I had won my buffalo, I had not noticed that I was far from every one else. No admiring friends were about, and as far as I could see I was on the plain alone. The herd of buffalo had completely disappeared. And as for father, much as I wished for him, he was out of sight and I had no idea where he was.

I stood and looked at the animal on the ground. I was happy. Every one must know that I, Ota K'te, had killed a buffalo. But it looked as if no one knew where I was, so no one was coming my way. I must then take something from this animal to show that I had killed it. I took all the arrows one by one from the body. As I took them out, it occurred to me that I had used five arrows. If I had been a skillful hunter, one arrow would have been sufficient, but I had used five. Here it was that temptation came to me. Why could I not take out two of the arrows and throw them away? No one would know, and then I should be more greatly admired and praised as a hunter. As it was, I knew that I should be praised by father and mother, but I wanted more. And so I was tempted to lie.

I was planning this as I took out my skinning knife that father had sharpened for me the night before. I skinned one side of the animal, but when it came to turning it over, I was too small. I was wondering what to do when I heard my father's voice calling, "To-ki-i-la-la-hu-wo," "Where are you?" I quickly jumped on my pony and rode to the top of a little hill near by. Father saw me and came to me at once. He was so pleased to see me and glad to know that I was safe. I knew that I could never lie to my father. He was too fond of me and I too proud of him. He had always told me to tell the truth. He wanted me to be an honest man, so I resolved then to tell the truth even if it took from me a little glory. He rode up to me with a glad expression on his face, expecting me to go back with him to his kill. As he came up, I said as calmly as I could, "Father, I have killed a buffalo." His smile changed to surprise and he asked me where my buffalo was. I pointed to it and we rode over to where it lay, partly skinned.

Father set to work to skin it for me. I had watched him do this many times and knew perfectly well how to do it myself, but I could not turn the animal over. There was a way to turn the head of the animal so that the body would be balanced on the back while being skinned. Father did this for me, while I helped all I could. When the hide was off, father put it on the pony's back with the hair side next to the pony. On this he arranged the meat so it would balance. Then he covered the meat carefully with the rest of the hide, so no dust would reach it while we traveled home. I rode home on top of the load.

I showed my father the arrows that I had used and just where the animal had been hit. He was very pleased and praised me over and over again. I felt more glad than ever that I had told the truth and I have never regretted it. I am more proud now that I told the truth than I am of killing the buffalo.

We then rode to where my father had killed a buffalo. There we stopped and prepared it for taking home. It was late afternoon when we got back to camp. No king ever rode in state who was more proud than I that day as I came into the village sitting high up on my load of buffalo meat. Mother had now two hunters in the family and I knew how she was going to make over me. It is not customary for Indian men to brag about their exploits and I had been taught that bragging was not nice. So I was very quiet, although I was bursting with pride. Always when arriving home I would run out to play, for I loved to be with the other boys, but this day I lingered about close to the tipi so I could hear the nice things that were said about me. It was soon all over camp that Ota K'te had killed a buffalo.

My father was so proud that he gave away a fine horse. He called an old man to our tipi to cry out the news to the rest of the people in camp. The old man stood at the door of our tipi and sang a song of praise to my father. The horse had been led up and I stood holding it by a rope. The old man who was doing the singing called the other old man who was to receive the horse as a present. He accepted the horse by coming up to me, holding out his hands to me, and saying, "Ha-ye," which means "Thank you." The old man went away very grateful for the horse.

That ended my first and last buffalo hunt. It lives only in my memory, for the days of the buffalo are over.

Pen Pals

by Michael Dorris

"DEAR Mohammed," I began my letter. "I'm very sorry but I am not able to send you a Kodak camera. However, I would still like to be your pen pal. How are things in Sierra Leone? Things here are fine."

Mohammed was the most persistently demanding of the five correspondents I maintained, at my peak, in Africa. The others— Margot (the youngest daughter of a Viennese Jewish family who had fled to Kampala, Uganda, just before the outbreak of World War II), Derek (an English-speaking white South African who lived in Pietermaritzburg on the Indian Ocean), Ali (a boy in Cairo who wanted to become an architect), and Anna (a high school student with perfect penmanship in Ibadan, Nigeria) were content to exchange occasional postcards, family photos, and canceled stamps.

We met each other through the services of the International Friendship League, an organization in Boston that, for a small fee, matched would-be letter writers from around the world. I had heard of the league's existence on a radio program when I was twelve, and sent in my money and a request for a pen pal in Europe who shared my interests in reading, history, and folk music. At the time, there was nobody nearby who seemed to care about any of those things, and I felt lonely and hopelessly weird. *Unpopular* is too kind a word to describe my status. I was the kind of kid who wore glasses from the second grade on and never took them off, the kind who got his homework in on the day it was due (sometimes typed), the kind who could not catch a ball even when it fell into his baseball glove. Everyone I knew seemed to be part of groups whose doors were closed to me, so I had plenty of time to daydream, to imagine traveling to far-off places, meeting interesting, exotic people, being appreciated for the fascinating individual I was sure I was.

The International Friendship League was my passport out of the town where I lived, my ticket to anywhere. Together with my first address—of a boy my age, also named Michael, who lived in London—I received a map of the world and a long scroll on which I could locate and list all contacts I made. There were fifty spaces for names, and, as I tacked the papers to the wall above my bed, I calculated that I had at least forty-nine friends to go. Before sleep I would browse the map and select the country from which I would seek my next pen pal. All I needed was a week's allowance, an airmail stamp, and the cooperation of the people in Boston, who never let me down.

Michael from England turned out to like mystery books, and sent one of his favorites along with his third letter. He was full of questions about America, about places and practices I took for granted, and answering him made me look at familiar things with a fresh perspective. My second pen pal, Ingrid, was from Sweden, and passionate about politics. She disapproved of some of the positions of the Social Democrats, the party in power in Stockholm, and through her vivid descriptions I grew to anticipate the next round of Scandinavian elections more eagerly than I did those in the United States. Ingrid demanded to know what progress was being made with the civil rights movement in this country and what I was doing about equal justice for the reservation. And her idealism was infectious.

The list on my wall began to fill; whenever I earned some extra money I went on a continental binge. One spring I splurged on South America, gaining as correspondents a soccer player in São Paulo, Brazil, a set of identical twins in Medellín, Colombia, and an aspiring radio announcer in Lima, Peru. Though they were friendly, their attitudes toward the United States, and toward me as a North American, were surprisingly cynical. I was forced to consider that in the eyes of our Southern Hemisphere neighbors, "we" were not always regarded favorably.

Tucked into each letter I received from Reiko in Tokyo was an origami figure, an intricately folded piece of paper fashioned to resemble a tiny animal. Masoud, in Tehran, supported the reform policies of the shah, and Jens, in Jakarta, was determined that I would at least learn to write a grammatical sentence in his language. Helen Scott from Melbourne wanted to be a nurse and move to Canada, and Veronica Nops from Auckland opposed atomic power. She invited me to visit her in New Zealand, and twenty years after our initial exchange of letters, I did.

During the seventh and eighth grades and throughout high school I became "known" at our local post office. When mail from Ireland appeared, regular and without fail, on the first and fifteenth of every month, Grace George, my postmistress, would ask after the health of Eileen's blind mother. When the first letter arrived from a new place, Grace would weigh the envelope in her hand before giving it to me. "India has a lot to say," she might comment on one day, and on the next, "Those Portuguese sure like to spend their money on stamps."

After a few years, the map above my bed was festooned with colored pins—orange for males, green for females. At its maximum extent, there were thirty-two names on my "active" list. My room was decorated with snapshots and postcards, with wall chimes from Finland and tapa cloth from Fiji, with a miniature Italian flag, and with a pebble collected on my Turkish pen pal's school trip to the archaeological site of Troy. I had more friends than anyone I knew, and was secure in their affections. I watched the international news on television with a proprietary eye—I was acquainted with people who would be affected by what happened in foreign lands—and I paid close attention to every important story on events in this country because I knew that within a week or so I would be called upon to explain, defend, or condemn it in twenty different letters.

My pen pals and I seemed to share the adventure of being young on the same planet, of conspiring together across the distances of geography and culture, of consoling our failures and believing in the infinite promise of our adult lives. We were a kind of International Friendship League without boundary, without flag. Through an exchange of addresses my pals began to correspond with each other, and, in the ensuing years, some of us have met, directly or indirectly. Helen, now a nurse in Hope, British Columbia, visited me in New York. My aunt went to Dublin and stopped in to see Eileen and her mother. Ingrid adopted a child from Ecuador and, during a layover, showed him off to Rudolfo, now a TV newsman in Lima.

Over time, some pen pals became so involved in their own lives that they gradually stopped writing, and others were silenced by more troubling circumstances. After the Islamic revolution in Iran I never heard again from Masoud, and Derek, from South Africa, has not answered my Christmas cards for years. The world turned out to be neither as simple nor as small as we once believed it to be. But even now, years after the intensity of our associations, I can't look at a globe without populating it, not with faceless mobs of people, but with those to whom I was once so tenuously connected, those whom in some small respect I came to know.

Because You're a Girl

by Dorothy Richardson and Don Yaeger

GROWING up, there were a lot of things I wasn't allowed to do or be a part of for one simple fact: I am a girl. That was frustrating because there was always one thing that came very natural to me, and that was athletics. I was always able to throw, catch, or kick any type of ball and be pretty good at it. It was actually a talent that I knew was a gift from God. I could feel it. Yet there were times when I was a little girl when I asked God why He gave me so much talent in an area with so few opportunities.

The frustration of being as good as the boys but unable to compete with them was made crystal clear when I was only 10 years old. My dad had just retired from the Air Force and we had moved back to Orlando. My brothers Kenny and Lonnie had joined little league baseball and I would go to all their games. One day, while waiting for one of their games to start, I was pitching to them. I loved it. In fact, I often dreamt about one day being a pitcher in the major leagues. Unbeknownst to me, I was being watched.

A coach walked over to me and commented on how impressed he was with my throwing arm. Then he asked if I would like to join his little league team. I couldn't believe it. These were the words I had been praying someone would one day say. But there was only one catch: He wanted me to cut my hair and answer to the name Bob. As quickly as I had gotten excited, I became crushed. I wanted to play, but I didn't want to pretend to be a boy just to get the chance. I told him, "Thanks but no thanks. If I have to hide who I am, I don't feel it's right."

When I asked my mother later why I couldn't play baseball just being me, she told me it was because the boys would feel bad when—not if—I struck them out and that their parents couldn't handle it when a girl struck their son out. I didn't know if she was right or not but it sure made me feel a little better. Her words showed she believed in me and my abilities. It was just the rest of the world that wasn't ready.

But at that moment, I was devastated. The feeling lasted, however, only for about five minutes. My brothers took off to their game. Then I met a friend of mine, Sunday Brown. She was a very talented athlete who was also denied the opportunity to play organized baseball. She and I walked over to a field nearby and started playing catch in the outfield. We had been playing catch for only a short while when a man came running up the right field foul line. I thought he was going to kick us off the field but instead he asked me if I had a few minutes to talk with a coach. I said sure, and started walking with him to the third base dugout. My first thought was, "not twice in one day."

As we walked past the infield, I noticed the players were not boys. They were women. Before reaching the dugout, a woman walked out to meet me and introduced herself. Boy, was I surprised when she said she was the coach of the Union Park Jets. She wanted to know if I had ever played softball. When I told her I hadn't, she informed me that softball wasn't so different from baseball. The ball was just a little bigger. I took a position at third and fielded a few ground balls. It's funny but already I felt like I belonged there.

The coach then called me back over and asked if I wanted to play on her team. Unbelievable! "Of course," I said. Then she asked how old I was. When I told her I was ten, she was stunned. You see this was an Amateur Softball Association *Women's* fast pitch Class A team. Most of the women on the team were in their twenties. She had a look on her face that I had seen many times before. Before any words came out of her mouth, I just knew another opportunity to play would pass me by. Instead, she said, "Well, let's go see your parents."

As we drove the mile from the park to my house, I prayed my parents would let me join the team. When we got out of the car, I led the coaches to the front door of the house. That just showed how serious this moment was, because we never used the front door except for very formal occasions. I introduced everyone, then just sat down and listened. It was out of my hands. After a number of questions and explanations, Mom and Dad said "yes" with one stipulation. I would have to put my glove up by my face while in the ready position if I played in the infield. "No problem," I said. I guess chipped teeth is one thing, but the thought of having them knocked out is another.

Up until that time in my life, I had felt I was a player without a team. Now I had found a team—or should I say, they had found me. And the best part was I could play as "Dorothy." What happened to me that day showed me that I did not have to compromise who I was and what I believed in, and that talent will be given a chance.

I often wondered why I was the one chosen and not Sunday.

She was a good athlete. The next few years provided the answer. Sunday Brown became the first girl to play baseball at the Union Park Downey Little League when Title IX provided the opportunity for girls to play with the boys if they wanted to. Who knows, if softball hadn't discovered me that year, I might have been playing baseball like Sunday. And maybe gunning for the Atlanta Braves instead of the Atlanta Olympics.

Realistically, the dream of playing in the major leagues was shattered the day I noticed how short-lived Sunday's baseball career was. There were no more opportunities for her after little league, whereas mine continued. At ten, I was already a part of the triple A of the major leagues of softball.

I learned early it doesn't matter how old you are—it matters how well you play. I became the starting third baseman and leadoff hitter for the Union Park Jets. I went from never having played softball to hitting off Class A fast pitches in the fifty to sixty miles per hour range. I fell in love with the sport.

Our uniforms were sharp. The colors were red, white, and blue. I remember they didn't have any shorts small enough to fit me, so my mom and I went shopping for a smaller pair. None of the shorts we found had a stripe on the side. The team's official shorts were red and had a thin red, white, and blue stripe down the sides. Mom and I searched everywhere for a similar stripe. But the only one we could find was wider. We bought it anyway and Mom sewed it onto the sides of my new uniform shorts. It didn't matter that they were different. I was proud to wear them because Mom had put the stripes on for me.

Just before the season started, my parents bought me my first glove, a Rawlings. It was beautiful. I call it my first official glove because I had been using my brother's up to that time. Now I was set . . . my Rawlings glove, my new uniform, and my shiny black Kangaroo metal cleats. I remember being so nervous before the games that I couldn't control the butterflies. In fact, it was a ritual to go to the bathroom before each game because the butterflies were out of control. They seemed to multiply the closer we were to game time. Even thinking about it now, I can still feel them. I was so excited to be able to play.

Baseball wasn't the only sport I didn't get a chance to play as a girl. When we lived in New Mexico, my older brother was on a football team. I actually thought about playing that sport. I was nine years old. I knew there was no way they would ever let me be the quarterback or a running back, which would be my favorite positions, but maybe, I thought, they'd let me be the punter. I loved kicking the football. It was something I was pretty good at, too. Coaches and players alike commented on how far I could kick the ball—much farther than any of the boys on the team—but when it came down to making the team, the length of my kicks didn't matter. Instead it always came down to the fact I was a girl.

Mother reminds me of how amazed she was when we lived in England and I was the regular goalie in my older brother's neighborhood soccer game. I was almost eight at the time and remember loving to play. Mom recalls worrying about me getting hurt playing with the older boys but said she realized I must have been good at it or they wouldn't be asking me to play. They accepted me as an equal because I had the ability to play the game. But the opportunity to play on the boys' organized soccer team didn't exist. Coaches said I wasn't allowed . . . because I'm a girl.

When I was younger there were times when I often thought I would have liked to have been born a boy. Not because I wanted to be one. I just wanted the opportunities they always seemed to have. It seemed that boys got to do everything that I wanted to do. And I wasn't able to play for reasons totally out of my control. It didn't seem right that if someone loved participating in a sport and had the talent to do it well they couldn't compete. If you told me I couldn't play because I was not fast enough, or I couldn't hit the ball well enough, or throw it hard enough, maybe I could say okay, I'll work on it. But when you tell me I cannot do something because of my gender, or my height, or my skin color, those are things I couldn't really change.

It didn't seem fair, but who do you complain to? You tell your mom it isn't fair, and she says "I know, honey, but life isn't always fair." The truth is my parents were very supportive. In fact, if it wasn't for them I wouldn't have been able to accomplish what I have. It was my dad who appointed me bat girl for my brothers' baseball team, which allowed me to practice with the boys and develop my skills. My parents recognized the talents God gave me and helped me seize what few opportunities were available. I believe that is why my parents gave me permission at such a young age to play on a women's fast-pitch softball team.

At the end of that first softball season with the Union Park Jets, I was named to the league's All-Star team. The team was going to Tennessee for a big tournament. A week before we were scheduled to leave, I was climbing some trees in the backyard. I had decided the best way to get down was to swing from one of the branches onto an old white Ford parked underneath the tree. Of course, I was barefooted. As I landed on the car, I lost my balance and fell backwards.

As I started to fall, I looked over my shoulder and saw some boards on the ground with nails sticking up from them. I gave an extra effort in the push off from the car and remember feeling that it was a great athletic move to push myself over the boards. I avoided the nails—but instead landed on an old rusty sickle. A sickle is like a machete with a long broomstick handle, used to cut tall weeds.

Immediately, I felt the sense of a cool breeze through my right foot. I looked down and all I could see was blood. The jagged edge had sliced my foot from the ball to the arch. My younger brother Lonnie and his friend helped me into the house. My older sister Kathy then drove me to the hospital. It took fifteen stitches to close the wound. No muscles or tendons were damaged. If I had landed on that sickle any other way, I could have lost a part of my foot. Because of the injury, I had to give up my position on the All-Star team that competed at the big tournament in Tennessee.

Instead, a few weeks later I hobbled my way up to the registration desk for the Orlando Rebels Instructional League. The Rebels were an Amateur Softball Association (ASA) Women's Major Fast-pitch League team. They competed at the highest level of fast pitch softball. The "Major Leagues" of our sport.

I was the last to arrive at the registration desk. Hundreds of girls were already inside C.L. Varner Stadium. Jean Daves, a Hall of Famer, was taking registrations. Mom filled out the form and handed it to Miss Daves. She glanced at it, and looking up at me she said, "You're too young." To be a part of the camp, you had to be twelve years old and I was still eleven. I felt my heart drop. Mom told her I would soon be twelve.

About this time the head coach and manager for the Orlando Rebels, Marge Ricker, walked over. She gave permission for me to register for the tryout. In later years, she told me she just didn't have the heart to say no to me. I was just standing there, a freckle-faced, scrawny little kid hobbling on one foot with a look of eagerness, wanting so desperately to play.

During the tryout, we were scheduled to go through different stations that demonstrated our skills in the fundamentals of the sport. The objective was to come up with teams that were evenly matched. But the ultimate goal of the instructional league was to teach fast-pitch softball to more girls and develop stronger talent in a "farm club" system for the Rebels.

Throughout the day, I didn't show very much. I could only run on the outside of my right foot because of the injury. In fact, I hobbled around the bases. I did manage to get a good distance on the throwing station but I didn't figure that impressed anyone. I was wrong. At the end of the day, I was chosen for an instructional team.

That night I realized I had been taught a valuable lesson—everything happens for a reason. No matter how disappointed you may get there is something good in store. I was heartbroken about missing the opportunity of playing as an All-Star in Tennessee. But because of the heartbreak, I was now being taught by All-Americans. Time would show that that painful accident was not a tragedy but a blessing for the future. Life can deal us very tough cards but God will not give you anything you cannot handle. At the time it makes no sense, but with time you see your growth.

After the instructional league ended, Mom got a phone call from Marge. They talked for a while, then Mom asked me if I wanted to be the bat girl for the Orlando Rebels. You bet I did! Marge had selected two of us from the instructional league to be bat girls for the following season. It was a girl named Bemmie and I.

I looked forward to spring training. As bat girls, we attended practices. Every Monday, Wednesday, and Friday from six to nine P.M. Bemmie and I mostly picked up equipment, but we also got to play catch and even shagged balls during batting practice. I would watch and study the skills of the players; even today you can see their influence on my style.

The season started on the last weekend of May, and culminated in mid August with the National Championship. Doubleheaders were played every Friday, Saturday, and Sunday. I tried to be the best bat girl I could be. I would concentrate on using good form and the proper fundamentals when playing catch with the left fielder. And when it was my turn to pick up the bats, I made it a challenge to pick them up as fast as I could. I was proud just to be a part of the Rebels.

But one fine summer evening, the pride of being a bat girl became the pride of being a softball player. During the second game of a doubleheader, we were beating Alabama 10-0 in the top of the sixth inning. Marge turned to Bemmie and me in the dugout and told us we were going into the game. I couldn't believe what I'd heard. At first, I didn't think she was serious. When I realized she wasn't kidding, I asked, "Is it legal?" Marge replied, "As bat girls you are on the official roster. It's legal. You two are going to hit this inning, then Dot, you go to right field. Bemmie, you're in left."

Everything good that could happen to a player in a game happened to me that night. I came up to bat with a runner on second. I got a base hit. The run scored, giving me an RBI. While on first, Marge gave me the sign to steal. I stole second base. When the next batter got a hit, Marge waved me around third. I beat the throw home and scored a run. On defense, I caught a routine fly ball for the first out. Later, I scooped up a line drive that was hit to me, then I threw the batter out at first to end the game. We had won, and I had played in the "major leagues." At the end of the game, Marge brought Bemmie and I back down to earth. "Get off cloud nine and start packing the bats," she said with a smile.

Later that week I wondered why I was put in right field. Maybe Marge put me there because I was not that good. Everybody knows the worst player is put in right field. Or so I thought. When I asked Marge what I needed to work on, she told me, "You must be kidding. The player with the best arm goes to right field." I learned a new appreciation for that position and the talent it requires.

That was the season of 1974. It also was the year the ASA National Championships for Women's Majors was held in Orlando, Florida. The Rebels were the host team. I got to observe the thrill of competition at the highest level. And of course as a bat girl, did so from the best seat in the house. At that tournament I met and got the autograph of Joan Joyce, a legend in her own time.

In the fall, I competed again in the Rebel instructional league. At the end of the season, I was selected for the newly formed Little Rebels, a fifteen and under girls softball team organized and coached by Marge herself. I was thirteen. One week later, Marge pulled me aside from a team meeting. We walked down the left field foul line toward third base and stopped for a minute. When we were far enough away from the rest of the team, she told me she had already spoken to my parents and they'd said the decision was up to me. She said, "Dot, you have the opportunity to play with the Big Rebels if you would like. But before you answer, realize you can stay with the Little Rebels and be a big frog in a little pond, or you can play with the Big Rebels and be a little frog in a big pond."

Without hesitation I said, "I want to be a little frog." I joined the Rebels that 1975 season and at thirteen years of age became the youngest player in history to play ASA Women's Major League Division.

Even though I was able to play softball with women twice my age, there still weren't many athletic opportunities for girls at Union Park Junior High. In fact, I had to be on the boys track team in seventh grade because there wasn't a girls team. The next year the school started having girls sports. When I look at the trophies I was awarded in Junior High, I am reminded of the evolution I've watched in sports. My seventh and eighth grade trophies had a male figure on the top. But by ninth grade, there seemed to be a little more acknowledgment of women because they had found trophies with a female figure.

During my ninth grade year, I played four sports: volleyball, basketball, softball, and track. The sports banquet held at the end of the year was a momentous evening. I had been selected as the Most Valuable Player in each of the four sports I played and became the first girl named as our school's Outstanding Athlete of the Year. There were four trophies and one beautiful plaque on the table before me. I remember after receiving the third trophy, I started hoping one of my teammates would be awarded the next.

But the school made sure I didn't get a big head. All the awards I received that night spelled my name D-O-R-T-H-Y, instead of D-O-R-O-T-H-Y.

By high school, there seemed to be more opportunities for girls to participate in athletics. I played five sports: volleyball, basketball, softball, track, and tennis, as well as continuing to play for the Orlando Rebels. It really wasn't as tough a transition as you might think. Each sport prepared me for the next. And each sport easily became my favorite. At school, we played slow-pitch softball. I couldn't believe we were having to play slow-pitch when colleges were giving scholarships for fast-pitch. I was fortunate that I was playing for the Orlando Rebels.

Some coaches wondered how I managed to play both without affecting my hitting. Well, Marge taught me how to hit left-handed when I was only 12. So for slow-pitch I hit from the right side of the plate and in fast-pitch from the left; therefore I didn't develop any bad habits.

I've always acknowledged the importance of education. It was encouraged in our home. We were taught to always do the best you could in every thing you did. That is the definition of a student-athlete. Not only was I All-Conference in every sport I played but I was also a member of the Junior National Honor Society, National Honor Society, Spanish Honor Society, and Dean's List.

The sports banquet my senior year at Colonial High School was as memorable as the one from my last year of junior high. I received the Most Valuable Player Award for each of the sports I'd played, but the coaches were undecided on how to handle the Outstanding Athlete of the Year Award. Previously it had only been given to a male athlete. My qualifications were unmatched. However, the decision was made to present dual awards to both a male and female athlete. That was seen as a disappointment by those who thought that I deserved the title alone. I was honored by those who'd argued for me. They made it possible for me to stand behind the podium and accept the award with a feeling of pride. It was the same award my older brother Kenny had received just three years earlier. He was in attendance with my parents. That night I was proud to recognize Kenny's accomplishments and his inspiration to me.

As I look back at my participation in sports during high school, it is interesting to analyze my decision not to run track until my senior year. The reason I didn't participate during my tenth and eleventh grades was because I got so nervous. Why? I was afraid of being beaten. Of losing the race. Of not being the fastest. It was so individualized, all my thoughts were about me, and I didn't like it. I put too much value on the result of the race instead of the competition. I grew up during those two years. I learned the importance of the challenge and the attempt to face it, not to hide from it. I learned, too, that your worth as a person does not lie in the win/loss column or in your batting average. Instead it lies within you and the things you do.

I joined the track team my senior year and loved it. I found a sense of security in who I was and the effort I gave, not in what others would think if I lost.

During the summers with the Orlando Rebels, I traveled the country playing softball. Our Rebels team was so incredibly talented that I seemed to learn something every time I took the field. It was like having fifteen mothers. We traveled in a motor home for road trips in the Atlanta Coast League and to Texas. Everyone would take turns as the driver or the copilot. Of course I could only be a copilot since I was too young to drive. I always slept in the bunk over the top of the driver and copilot. It was a small area, but perfect for me.

I remember being so excited about playing the upcoming games that I couldn't sleep at night. I would count the white striped lines dividing the road, the whole time listening to the eight track tapes we kept on the bus. The team favorites: the Stylistics and the Best of Bread, played over and over again. Even today when I hear those songs I can sing every word.

We played against the Stratford Raybestos Brakettes, the Atlanta Loreli Ladies, the Waltham Drifters, the Allentown Patriots, and the Bridgeport Coeds, to name a few. I'll never forget my first trip to play against the Raybestos Brakettes. It would be my first time facing the "living legends." We drove up to this gorgeous stadium, the Raybestos Memorial Field. The parking lot was full and the stands packed with four thousand people. One of the most embarrassing moments in my life happened before that game. As we ran out to take infield I tripped over the shoelaces of my brand-new cleats. I fell to the ground. I got up so fast I doubt anyone even saw me. If you blinked, you would have missed it.

It was that game when I first faced Joan Joyce. You know someone is good when you can remember how you performed against them. I got a hit the first time up to bat against Joyce. When I was on first base I looked in the dugout and every one of my teammates was busting up laughing, mostly in disbelief that this kid had gotten a hit off the legend. I'll never forget it. A hit up the middle. Our celebration was short-lived, however, as none of us touched the ball for the rest of the game. Joyce was a true competitor and she simply decided that my hit would be the last of the evening.

Imagine being on the road playing softball at thirteen years of age. We were given five dollars a day for meal money. Five dollars! That was a lot of money to me. I had never been given meal money before so it was a big deal. It was great but I did some crazy things. I had a chocolate milkshake for breakfast, lunch, and dinner for an entire three weeks on a road trip. When I came back home I had pimples all over my face. I broke out from all the chocolate. Another time I ate six doughnuts for breakfast and couldn't move without feeling sick. Not much nutrition there either.

During that first year with the Rebels, many of the players I admired, like Snookie Mulder and Kathy Stilwell, left the Rebels to form a new team called the Orlando Suns. Their absence created openings in the roster, and that's how I was given the opportunity to become a starter. I was the leadoff batter and re-sumed my place in right field.

I truly loved my position in the outfield. Warm-ups were espe-cially fun for me, as I had the opportunity to throw the ball to each consecutive base. One night, when I gunned the ball to third on a line shot, everyone in the stands—fifteen hundred people—stood up and gave me a standing ovation. In a warm-up! To me, it was just a warm-up throw, but that is how aston-ished people were at a thirteen-year-old playing in the women's majors.

After one of my first games, I was asked "How old do you feel when you play?" I said, "I never think of age. It does not really matter how old you are, it matters how well you play." The re-porter didn't like my answer and repeated the question. "Ok," I said. "I feel 21."

In 1976, the Women's Professional Fast-pitch softball league was formed, backed and supported by Billie Jean King. There were teams throughout the country. I was on the protected list of the Connecticut Falcons, though it didn't matter to me. I did not want to play professionally because I wanted to participate in the Olympics. I didn't know when but I knew I wanted it to happen more than anything.

By playing for the Rebels, I was able to be part of the real growth in women's softball. For that, I have to say thanks to that Little League baseball coach who wanted a pitcher named Bob.

The Bike

by Gary Soto

MY first bike got me nowhere, though the shadow I cast as I pedaled raced along my side. The leaves of bird-filled trees stirred a warm breeze and litter scuttled out of the way. Our orange cats looked on from the fence, their tails up like antennas. I opened my mouth, and wind tickled the back of my throat. When I squinted, I could see past the end of the block. My hair flicked like black fire, and I thought I was pretty cool riding up and down the block, age five, in my brother's hand-me-down shirt.

Going up and down the block was one thing, but taking the first curve, out of sight of Mom and the house, was another. I was scared of riding on Sarah Street. Mom said hungry dogs lived on that street, and red anger lived in their eyes. Their throats were hard with extra bones from biting kids on bikes, she said.

But I took the corner anyway. I didn't believe Mom. Once she had said that pointing at rainbows caused freckles, and after a rain had moved in and drenched the streets, after the sparrows flitted onto the lawn, a rainbow washed over the junkyard and reached the dark barrels of Coleman pickle. I stood at the window, looking out, amazed and devious, with the devilish horns of my butch haircut standing up. From behind the window, I let my finger slowly uncurl like a bean plant rising from earth. I uncurled it, then curled it back and made a fist. I should remember this day, I told myself.

I pedaled my squeaky bike around the curve onto Sarah Street, but returned immediately. I braked and looked back at where I had gone. My face was hot, my hair sweaty, but nothing scary seemed to happen. The street had looked like our street: parked cars, tall trees, a sprinkler hissing on a lawn, and an old woman bending over her garden. I started again, and again I rode the curve, my eyes open as wide as they could go. After a few circle eights I returned to our street. There ain't no dogs, I told myself. I began to think that maybe this was like one of those false rainbow warnings.

I turned my bike around and rode a few times in front of our house, just in case Mom was looking for me. I called out, "Hi Mom. I haven't gone anywhere." I saw her face in the window, curlers piled high, and she waved a dish towel at me. I waved back, and when she disappeared, I again tore my bike around the curve onto Sarah Street. I was free. The wind flicked my hair and cooled my ears. I did figure eights, rode up the curbs and onto lawns, bumped into trees, and rode over a garden hose a hundred times because I liked the way the water sprang up from the sprinkler after the pressure of my tires. I stopped when I saw a kid my age come down a porch. His machinery for getting around was a tricycle. Big baby, I thought, and said, "You can run over my leg with your trike if you want." I laid down on the sidewalk, and the kid, with fingers in his mouth, said, "OK."

He backed up and slowly, like a tank, advanced. I folded my arms behind my head and watched a jay swoop by with what looked like a cracker in its beak, when the tire climbed over my ankle and sparks of pain cut through my skin. I sat up quickly, my eyes flinging tears like a sprinkler.

The boy asked, "Did it hurt?"

"No," I said, almost crying.

The kid could see that it did. He could see my face strain to hold back a sob, two tears dropping like dimes into the dust. He pedaled away on his bucket of bolts and tossed it on his front lawn. He looked back before climbing the stairs and disappeared into the house.

I pulled up my pants leg. My ankle was purple, large and hot, and the skin was flaked like wood shavings. I patted spit onto it and laid back down. I cried because no one was around, the tears stirring up a lather on my dirty face. I rose to my feet and walked around, trying to make the ankle feel better. I got on my bicycle and pedaled mostly with the good leg. The few tears still on my eyelashes evaporated as I rode. I realized I would live. I did nothing fancy on the way home, no figure eights, no wiggling of the handlebars, no hands in my pockets, no closed eye moments.

Then the sudden bark of a dog scared me, and my pants leg fed into the chain, the bike coming to an immediate stop. I tugged at the cuff, gnashed and oil-black, until ripping sounds made me quit trying. I fell to the ground, bike and all, and let the tears lather my face again. I then dragged the bike home with the pants leg in the chain. There was nothing to do except lie in the dirt because Mom saw me round the corner from Sarah Street. I laid down when she came out with the belt, and I didn't blame the dog or that stupid rainbow.

First Wings

by Nancy Shore

"THERE are two kinds of stones," Amelia Earhart once wrote, "one of which rolls. Because I selected a father who was a railroad man it has been my fortune to roll."

In the summer of 1920, Earhart "rolled" out to the West Coast and into her parents' large Los Angeles house. The senior Earharts were supplementing their income by renting out rooms, one of them to Samuel Chapman, a young chemical engineer from Massachusetts. Chapman was immediately drawn to Earhart's ready wit and level, gray-eyed gaze. The attraction was mutual, and the pair soon began to spend their leisure hours together.

Earhart was also attracted to southern California and its wide variety of outdoor sports. She was, as she later said, "fond of automobiles, tennis, horseback riding, and almost anything that is active and carried out in the open." She and Chapman swam and played tennis, attended plays and political meetings together, and spent long hours talking about books and world affairs. Amy and Edwin Earhart liked Sam Chapman; they assumed that their daughter would marry him and become a conventional, contented housewife. They did not, it seems, know her as well as they thought.

The leisure-time activity Earhart enjoyed most was not one she shared with Chapman. She had never forgotten the excitement she had experienced at the flying field in Toronto, and now she found herself irresistibly drawn to the airfields that had sprung up around Los Angeles.

In 1920 aviation was still something of a novelty. Airshows were a popular pastime; on weekends crowds jammed the airfields to watch retired army pilots "stunt" in old warplanes. Earhart went to her first air meet—where the sky, she later recalled, "was a perfect blue"—with her father. Entranced by the sight of the little planes soaring and diving through the air, she asked her father to inquire about the price of flying lessons. He returned with a discouraging report: local pilots charged $1,000 to teach a student to fly. For the Earharts, scraping along on what was left of the Otis legacy, it was an impossible sum.

Amelia Earhart, however, was not easily daunted. She wanted to fly, and fly she would. A few days later she paid a professional pilot $1 for a 10-minute ride over Hollywood. From that moment on, she was committed to the air.

*

"I think I'd like to learn to fly," Amelia announced casually that night at dinner with her parents.

Her father, perhaps assuming his daughter was voicing a passing fancy, responded just as casually. "Not a bad idea," he said. "When do you start?"

She started at once. As a first step, she signed up for lessons on credit. She was confident that somehow or other the bill would be paid, but her father was dismayed. Faced with the reality of the lessons, he told her he simply could not afford them.

"Evidently he thought that if he didn't pay I wouldn't fly," Earhart wrote later, "but I was determined." To finance the lessons, she got her first paying job, sorting mail for the telephone company in Los Angeles. From then on, she later recalled, "the family scarcely saw me. I worked all week and spent what I had of Saturday and Sunday at the airport."

The airfield was on the outskirts of town; to get there meant an hour's streetcar ride followed by a walk of several miles along a dusty highway. In those early days of aviation, serious fliers dressed the part in semimilitary outfits. Wanting to be as inconspicuous as possible in an arena dominated by men, Earhart cropped her hair and donned breeches, boots, and a man's leather jacket. She reveled in the romantic atmosphere of the makeshift airfield with its ramshackle hangars and secondhand planes.

Her flight instructor was Neta Snook, a fine pilot and the first woman to graduate from the prestigious Curtiss School of Aviation. Snook insisted that her eager pupil learn the name and function of every part of the training plane before going aloft. The trainer, a Curtiss Canuck biplane, had dual controls, a safety device that enabled an instructor to override decisions made by a student in the air. With Snook in the rear cockpit, Earhart practiced takeoffs and landings. When Snook was satisfied that her student had mastered these basics, she began to teach her various aerial maneuvers and stunt-flying techniques.

A thorough knowledge of "stunting" is essential to pilots; it prepares them to cope with any emergency that may arise in flight. "The fundamental stunts are tips, stalls, spins, loops, barrels and rolls," explained Earhart in her book *Last Flight*. "Unless a pilot has actually recovered from a stall, has actually put his plane into a spin and brought it out he cannot know accurately what these acts entail."

Earhart spent as much time as she could with the other pilots at the airfield. Trying to learn everything there was to know about aviation, she asked innumerable questions and listened avidly as the experienced fliers talked "shop." She already knew a fair amount about motors from her class in automobile repair but she knew she needed to learn much more. These pilots, most of whom had flown during World War I, had picked up their techniques the hard way. They were experts at night flying, staying on course over unfamiliar territory, changing direction or speed quickly.

The veteran pilots found Earhart good-natured, unpretentious, and quick to learn. She would crawl under a plane, make repairs, and, covered with grease, emerge smiling happily. She was, concluded the airfield crowd, "a natural."

At last the time came for her to solo. She went up 5,000 feet and, as she put it, "played around a little and came back." Although she made a less than perfect landing, she was thrilled. "It's so breathtakingly beautiful up there," she said. "I want to fly whenever I can." And she wanted a plane of her own. She started saving money, willing to forego all luxuries until she could afford her heart's desire.

Her first solo flight behind her, Earhart signed up for advanced flying lessons. She went to work in a photography studio to pay for them. Later she was to write, "I've had 28 different jobs in my life and I hope I'll have 28 more. Experiment! Meet new people. That's better than any college education. By adventuring about, you become accustomed to the unexpected. The unexpected then becomes what it really is—the inevitable."

Flying, which had begun as a casual interest, was rapidly developing into an obsession for Earhart. Her father considered her pastime dangerous and foolish, but her mother was enthusiastic, even after her daughter had made two crash landings. The first time, a rainstorm had forced her down in a farmer's meadow, leaving her suspended upside down by her safety belt. Flung from the cockpit during her second forced landing, this one in a weedy field, she again emerged unhurt. Amy Earhart was calm in both cases. She said that when her daughter did things "she always did them very carefully. . . . She thought it out and her mind was quick and I had no special anxiety."

By 1922 Earhart had given up her plans to return to college.

She continued to spend much of her free time with Sam Chapman and her parents still assumed the pair would marry. Marriage, however, was not on Earhart's list of priorities. That summer she received a pilot's license from the Federation Aeronautique Internationale, the only agency that issued licenses at the time. She was now one of the few women in the world licensed to fly.

On July 24, 1922, Amelia Earhart was 25 years old; her birthday present—paid for with her own savings and generous contributions from her mother and sister—was an airplane, a bright yellow Kinner Canary. It was secondhand, and its single, 60-horsepower engine sent rough vibrations through its cockpit, but Earhart thought it was wonderful. "Immediately," she wrote, "I found that my whole feeling of flying changed." In exchange for free hangar space, she worked for aircraft manufacturer W.G. Kinner, demonstrating the plane to prospective buyers.

Edwin Earhart and his two daughters attended an air meet at Los Angeles's Rogers Field in October 1922. As he and his younger daughter anxiously scanned the sky, his older daughter rapidly disappeared from view, soaring aloft in her Kinner Canary. When the small yellow plane landed an hour later, the airfield's loudspeakers boomed out the news: Amelia Earhart had climbed to a height of 14,000 feet, breaking the women's altitude record.

That record was soon overtaken by well-known aviator Ruth Nichols; it is nonetheless memorable for being the earliest of Earhart's many aviation "firsts." She made an effort to break the new record a few weeks later. Taking her plane up to 12,000 feet, she ran into a dense bank of clouds; with snow stinging her face as she sat in the Canary's open cockpit she found herself flying blind through an airy limbo. Undaunted, she continued to climb. When the snow turned to sleet, however, she knew it was time to abandon the effort, at least for the moment. She kicked the rudder and sent the plane into a downward spin. Zooming through the fog, she leveled off at 3,000 feet and landed safely.

"What the hell were you trying to do?" shouted another pilot. "If the fog had closed in completely all the way down to the ground we would have had to dig you out in pieces!"

"I suppose you would have," said Earhart coolly. She was, in fact, thoroughly shaken by the harrowing flight, but she had no intention of letting any of the men on the field know it.

from

Babe Didrikson: The World's Greatest Woman Athlete

by Gene Schoor

IT was the evening before one of the biggest track events of the decade—the National AAU championships in Illinois, which would qualify the individual winners for the 1932 Olympics.

In her downtown Chicago hotel room, marking time for the biggest moment of her life, twenty-one-year-old Mildred "Babe" Didrikson was a bundle of nerves. She paced up and down the room. She bounced from one chair to another. She got down on the floor to practice the correct form for the start of her sprint and hurdle races. "Hands placed shoulder-width apart, thumb and fingers pressed into the floor, squat down on your toes." A dozen times Babe tried her starting position and then bounced up as an imaginary starter's gun barked.

Finally Mrs. Henry Wood, her chaperone and companion looked sternly across the room at the thin-faced young girl, now down on the floor practicing another exercise.

"Babe, you're as tight and nervous as a cat burglar, so stop your fidgeting or you'll wear us both out before the races begin tomorrow. Come on; let's go right out and buy you a new hat. A young girl needs a new hat, especially on her very first trip to Chicago."

"A new hat? Why shucks, I never had a hat before. Anyhow, I can't afford a new hat. I only have three dollars."

"I'll buy the hat," said Mrs. Wood. "It's my gift for you."

The Babe was thrilled. Here she was in Chicago for the first time, her first hat, and tomorrow the biggest day of her life—the National AAU track meet.

Mrs. Wood and Babe visited several millinery shops before Babe spotted a hat that she wanted—a pink felt hat with a cluster of tiny flowers.

"It's just the right hat for you, Babe," said Mrs. Wood.

"Gosh, it looks great," said Babe. "I'll never take it off."

Back at the hotel once more, Mrs. Wood ordered Babe to bed.

"It's late and we have a long drive to the stadium, so let's get some sleep—and take off your new hat, please."

But sleep did not come quickly that night. Babe Didrikson was too excited.

Mrs. Wood heard Babe tossing in her bed and moaning.

"Anything wrong, Babe?" she asked.

"I just can't fall asleep."

"Why don't you close your eyes and think of something pretty?" suggested Mrs. Wood. "Think of your hat, some nice young fellow back home. Just get your mind off the meet. You'll be asleep soon enough."

For a moment, the Babe lay still. Then she rolled and tossed about again.

"I've got these pains in my stomach," she said.

Mrs. Wood was out of her bed, fast. She switched on the lights in the room.

"Where does it hurt?"

"Right here," said Babe, putting her hand down on where the pains were sharpest.

"Your right side!" said Mrs. Wood. "I'd better get a doctor!"

"No! No doctor!" pleaded the Babe.

But Mrs. Wood was already at the telephone.

"You'll need a doctor! It may be your appendix!"

The doctor was up in the room in no time. He was kind and patient as his fingers probed the sore spots.

"Does this hurt?" he asked.

"No," said the Babe.

"Does this hurt?" asked the doctor, his fingers moving.

The young girl shook her head.

"Well," said the doctor, gently covering the young girl with her blanket, "there's really nothing wrong with you that I can find."

"But I had these severe pains," protested the Babe.

"You don't have them now, do you?" asked the kind old gentleman.

The Babe shook her head.

"Not now."

"Just nerves," said the doctor.

He turned to Mrs. Wood, who was still pulling on her fingers in nervous anticipation.

"She's just excited," said the doctor. "The excitement is affecting the nerve center in her diaphragm."

"Thank you, doctor," said Mrs. Wood, considerably relieved.

"I could give her a sedative," suggested the doctor, "to quiet her down."

"No pills," said the Babe. "I've got that big meet tomorrow."

"You might take a lukewarm bath; that might help you relax," said the doctor.

Babe took the advice and soaked herself in a hot, sudsy bath. It did calm her nerves and settle her down, but it wasn't until almost morning, however, before either Babe or Mrs. Wood could fall asleep.

Neither could recall how long they slept, but it was a sound sleep and much longer than they had intended.

The Babe woke up first.

She looked around the strange room for just a moment before she realized where she was. Then, suddenly, she looked at her watch. It was late in the morning, perhaps too late for her to get to the track meet in Evanston in time for the first event.

"Mrs. Wood!" she called. "We're awful late!"

She was out of bed.

So was Mrs. Wood.

They rushed to get dressed.

"Just throw your track things in your bag!" said Mrs. Wood.

They hurried out of the hotel and into the street. There was a cab there, waiting in front of the hotel doors. They climbed into it.

"Dyche Stadium!" ordered Mrs. Wood.

"That's in Evanston," said the cabbie.

"We know it's in Evanston," said Mrs. Wood. "Hurry! We're late!"

"Relax, we're on our way," said the cabbie.

Traffic was heavy.

"Can't you hurry?" pleaded Mrs. Wood.

"Sorry," said the cabbie, "I'm going as fast as I can."

Mrs. Wood turned to the Babe.

"There won't be time for you to dress at the field," she said. "You'd better dress right here. I'll hold this blanket up around you. Get into your track suit."

There was a crowd of athletes on the field, each club with ten or twelve or more contestants for the events of the afternoon.

Then the announcer roared, "Here is the one-woman track team from the Employers Casualty Insurance Company of Dallas. Babe Didrikson!"

Babe Didrikson, dressed in her natty blue-and-white track outfit, trotted to the center of the stadium, a broad smile on her face, waving enthusiastically to the crowd.

For just a split second there was a stunned surprise among the spectators as they watched the solitary representative from Texas move out into the sun. Then a wild cheer rose up from the stands. The sheer courage of a girl who single-handedly would compete for a post on the Olympics squad in competition with the finest teams in the nation got to the crowd like a shot of adrenalin. And they responded, as it always does to the man or the woman battling the impossible odds. The huge crowd thundered to its feet, roaring their support. They chanted her name continuously throughout that record-breaking afternoon.

"It brought out goose bumps all over me," said Babe Didrikson, speaking of her welcome at Dyche Stadium that afternoon. "I can feel the bumps now, just thinking about that unbelievable day."

The hometown support always seems to get the adrenalin flowing faster in the blood of an athlete and, for all purposes, the cheers at Evanston gave Babe Didrikson the feeling that she was performing before a hometown crowd. At least that is the way she responded on that July afternoon in 1932.

She was like a Greek goddess, like someone possessed, as she moved from the 80-meter hurdles to the high jump, from the high jump to the 100-meter dash, from the 100-meter dash to the javelin throw.

She kept going. From the javelin throw she hurried to the 8-pound shot put. From the shot put she moved to the broad-jump pit. From the broad jump she dashed over to throw the discus. After she threw the discus she was ready for the baseball throw. It was almost impossible to keep up with her, but the Babe kept going as the cheers from the stands grew louder and louder.

She would stop briefly to change her shoes or take a swallow of water. Mrs. Wood would hand her a towel between the separate heats, and the Babe would quickly dry her face and hands. Mrs. Wood would give her a swallow of orange juice, and the Babe was off again for another heat of the hurdles, or the sprints, or the discus toss, the high jump, the broad jump. She was a human dynamo all over the field that afternoon.

There was good reason to cheer this incredible display of ability, for there never had been an exhibition of athletic prowess . . . courage . . . determination and all-around excellence to match Babe Didrikson's performance that sunny afternoon as she triumphed over one champion after another in almost every contest she entered.

Babe seemed to have mystical powers that day. Of the eight events she entered, the 100-yard dash was the only event in which she failed to score a single point. She had rarely performed in the shot put or the discus. On this incredible day, she defeated shot-put champion Rena MacDonald with a toss of 39 feet, 6¼ inches. She placed fourth in the discus to gain one point. Next she won the baseball throw, with a throw of 272 feet, 2 inches, breaking her own record for the event. She captured first place in the running broad jump with a leap of 17 feet, 6 inches. She threw the javelin 139 feet, 3 inches, which bettered her own world record. She then ran her first heat in the 80-meter hurdles in 11.9 seconds, another world record.

In the high jump she was up against another outstanding competitor, Jean Shiley, a high-jump champion from Temple University. Both Jean Shiley and the Babe cleared the bar at 5 feet, 3⅛ inches. This was the record at the time, held by Fräulein M. Gisolf of the Netherlands. The bar was lifted another sixteenth of an inch. Jean Shiley cleared it. So did Babe Didrikson.

The bar was lifted once more, another sixteenth of an inch. The Babe couldn't make it. But neither could Jean Shiley. It was another first place for Babe Didrikson, a tie with Jean Shiley, but first place anyway.

The Babe had entered eight events. She won five of those events. She tied for first place in the high jump. In addition, she took fourth place in the discus and just missed scoring in the 100-meter dash as she placed fourth.

It was an unforgettable display. She had won six gold medals and broken four world records in the space of three hours in a single afternoon.

Perhaps even more remarkable was the fact that this slim young girl had piled up 30 points for her team, the Employers Casualty Insurance Company of Dallas. Babe Didrikson, of course, was the entire team.

The Illinois Women's Athletic Club of Chicago, with twenty-two representatives on the field, was second with 22 points.

The Western Women's Club of San Francisco was third with 13 points.

The Meadowbrook Club of Philadelphia was fourth with 9 points.

"Babe, the twenty-one year old lass, who works as a clerk in the Employers Casualty Insurance Company at Dallas," wrote the reporter for the New York *Times*, "today single-handedly won the National Amateur Athletic Union's championship in track and field for her club and reserved for herself three places on the U.S. Olympic squad."

"It was a victory," he continued, "without equal in the history of sport and will rank for all time as one of the truly remarkable performances ever accomplished by a single performer."

George Kirksey, covering the events for the United Press, wrote of the Babe, "It was the most amazing series of performances ever accomplished by any individual, male or female, in track and field history."

Paul Gallico, sports editor of the New York *Daily News*, and later to become one of the best-selling authors of all time, said after witnessing her performance in Evanston, "I cannot think of any male athlete with the possible exception of Jim Thorpe who had come even close to spread-eagling a track meet all by himself, the way young Babe Didrikson did at the Dyche Stadium."

"You did it! You did it!" screamed a hysterically happy Mrs. Henry Wood as the Babe came off the field, tired and sweaty. "You won the meet all by yourself!"

"Let's celebrate," said the Babe, simply.

"You must be too tired," protested Mrs. Wood. "We'll just get you back to the hotel. You'll just shower up and rest!" persisted Mrs. Wood.

"And then we'll celebrate," said young Babe Didrikson.

They did.

That night, some friends in Chicago took them out and they danced till three in the morning.

The next day, Babe loosened her muscles with a fast workout in Dyche Stadium.

"I don't want my muscles to tighten up," she explained to Mrs. Wood. "Besides, I've got to be in shape for all those foreign track stars. After all, I told my daddy when I was a small girl of ten that I would win the Olympic championship for the United States, and I've got to make good on that promise."

from

Wait Till Next Year

by Doris Kearns Goodwin

A BLACK delivery van pulled up to the front entrance of the house next door. My parents and I watched from the window as a uniformed driver dismounted, opened the gate of the van, and wheeled a large wooden crate toward the visibly excited assemblage of the Goldschmidt family standing at the front door.

Television had come to the neighborhood.

That night, the parents and children of Southard Avenue crowded into the Goldschmidts' living room, and watched as vaguely defined, snowy figures cavorted across the seven-inch black-and-white screen embedded in an odd block of furniture. "A marvel," the adults assured one another, as Mr. Goldschmidt continually adjusted the metal rod of the antenna. But to me and my playmates, it was only another wonder in a world of constantly unfolding wonders, like the stories my mother told me, the first book I read, or my first trip to Ebbets Field.

When the Goldschmidts bought their television in 1946, there were only seven thousand sets in use in the entire country, and theirs was the only one on our block. Within months, the number doubled when the Lubars' living room became the home of a nine-inch set with a slightly better picture, which became an irresistible attraction for all the children on the block. Almost every afternoon we would congregate on the Lubars' front stoop, waiting expectantly, and often vocally, for the invitation to enter, so we could sit cross-legged on the floor and watch the amazing parade of puppets, comedians, and cowboys which marched across their tiny screen.

It was only a matter of time, spurred by embarrassment at our imposition on the Lubars, before every family on our block had a set. And the pattern in our neighborhood, where desire begot what seemed like necessity, was repeated across America. By 1950, there were sets in three million homes; from then on, sales grew at a rate of five million a year, until, by the end of the decade, more than fifty million families would own a television.

When our own ten-inch table console finally arrived, my

parents invited everyone on the block to come over for a Sunday-afternoon showing of *The Super Circus.* That morning, my mother set out hot dog rolls and hamburger buns, prepared a salad, put extra chairs in the living room for the grown-ups, and laid a blanket on the floor for the children. The entrance of the handsome ringmaster into the center ring, dressed in a sequined costume, was greeted by a low, admiring whistle from Elaine's grandmother, and the circus began. We giggled at the antics of the clowns, marveled at the sight of the stately lions, and gasped at the daring of the high-wire artists.

To me, the afternoon was more memorable and exciting than my trip to see the actual Ringling Brothers Circus in Madison Square Garden. But not because of television. As a result of my mother's illness, I almost never had a group of friends at my home, to say nothing of the entire neighborhood. On this Sunday, however, I was a hostess, bringing someone a second hot dog, refilling the bowl of potato chips, constantly looking around to see what needs I could fill. Even though everyone was looking at the television set, I felt as if I were on stage, playing a role I thoroughly enjoyed. As soon as the show was over, and the guests departed, I asked my mother if we could do this every week, making our house the center of Sunday activity. "I'm sorry," my mother said, "but I simply can't do it. Even now, I am so exhausted just from having everyone here that I've got to lie down for a little while. But I'll tell you what, if you'd like to pick one show each week and have all the kids over to see it, I think that would be fine."

I picked *Howdy Doody,* my favorite show, featuring a freckled puppet in a plaid shirt, dungarees, and cowboy boots; an affable ventriloquist, Buffalo Bob, in fringed buckskin; and a "Peanut Gallery," composed of the luckiest kids in the world. At 5:25 p.m., we gathered before the set, staring at NBC's test pattern for five minutes before Buffalo Bob's booming voice opened the show: "Say, kids, what time is it?" "It's Howdy Doody Time," we shrieked in reply. The pitch of excitement continued as Clarabell the clown sneaked up behind Buffalo Bob to shoot water in his face, and we laughed so hard our stomachs hurt. Only when Buffalo Bob said good night and the kids in the Peanut Gallery waved goodbye did we finally calm down, and my friends disperse for dinner.

When the Friedles bought their thirteen-inch console, we flocked to their house on Tuesday evenings to watch Milton Berle; the Lubars' house became our scheduled stop for the

Saturday-morning cartoons. We gathered to watch TV's first interplanetary heroes: Tom Corbett, Captain Video, and Superman. I was visiting Eileen Rust when their television set arrived. The box was unimpressive, and Eileen began to cry, fearing that her set would have the smallest screen in the neighborhood. We watched as the carton was opened to reveal a giant eighteen-inch set, the largest on the block. Eileen gasped and the rest of us began to clap. Suddenly, Eileen's house became the most desirable place to gather.

Television entered our lives robed as the bearer of communal bonds, providing a new set of common experiences, block parties, and festive gatherings shared by children and adults alike. The fantasies of television slowly infiltrated our own. After the first soap operas, *Search for Tomorrow* and *Love of Life,* appeared on the air in the fall of 1951, our mothers could be found in spirited conversation discussing the behavior of their favorite characters and debating the likely outcome of their latest difficulties as if they were another family on the block. For days, our parents discussed the dramatic reaction of Elaine's seventy-five-year-old great-grandmother, Amelia, to the kidnapping of the little girl, Patti, on *Search for Tomorrow.* Patti was the six-year-old daughter of Joanne Barron, a young widow whose rich in-laws had kidnapped the child after losing a custody battle. A desperate week-long chase ended as police helped Joanne pursue the child's kidnappers through woods, which, in the early days of live television, consisted simply of a dark area filled with a maze of music stands affixed with branches to represent trees. Finding Patti's shoes near a pond, the searchers feared she had drowned, though viewers knew she was still alive in the hands of her evil grandmother.

At this point in the drama, Amelia, her print housedress flapping, her white hair disheveled, came rushing into the street, alarm in her voice. She demanded that we call the police and tell them where Patti was. By doing nothing, she insisted, we were endangering the life of this lovely child. Futilely, our mothers tried to explain that the show was a fictional drama, that Joanne and her daughter were actresses following a script. But Amelia refused to believe it, and we could do nothing to assuage her anxiety until the next episode, when Patti was found and returned to her mother.

The confusion of television with reality was not limited to the very old. One evening, my television screen revealed Joan of Arc being burned at the stake. There, before my eyes, the young woman stood, lashed to a piling atop a pyre in the old market-place in Rouen, France. A male voice denounced her as a heretic who must pay for her sins with her life. She was, he said, like a rotten branch that must be severed to preserve the tree. "It is not true," Joan cried. "I am a good Christian." Her words went unheeded. The fire crackled and the flames consumed her. Stunned by this violence taking place in front of me, I raced into the kitchen to find my mother. She reassured me that no one was being hurt, that the program was simply one of a series of historical dramatizations, called *You Are There,* narrated by Walter Cronkite. Through re-enactments and "eyewitness" accounts, the series endeavored to provide viewers with a sense that they were actually present at important moments in history. My anxiety was replaced by embarrassment at my naïveté, and I returned to the screen. In the weeks that followed, I watched the capture of John Wilkes Booth, the siege of the Alamo, the fall of Fort Sumter, the signing of the Declaration of Independence, the surrender of Robert E. Lee at Appomattox, and the duel between Hamilton and Burr.

For me, however, the flow of drama and entertainment was of small consequence beside the glorious opportunity to watch my Dodgers on the screen. In 1951, for the first time, I could follow the Dodgers for a full season on television. I watched Gil Hodges stretch to snag a skidding grounder and throw to the pitcher covering first; saw Carl Furillo as he barehanded a ball that bounced off the rightfield wall and then fired to second to catch a runner trying to extend a single into a double; and glimpsed the smile flicker across Robinson's face as he crossed home plate with the winning run.

Meeting
New Challenges

The Crown

by Russell Baker

RUSSELL BAKER
*Russell Baker, a noted humorist and observer of modern life,
started his writing career working for the* Baltimore Sun *and*
The New York Times. *His "Observer" column has appeared in
the* Times *since 1962. Mr. Baker won the Pulitzer Prize in
1979 for his column, and in 1983 for his book* Growing Up. *Mr.
Baker's work is important in that he has taken newspaper-
style writing to a higher, more literary level.*

I ROSE at four-thirty that morning and started dressing in
white tie and tails. It was still pitch black outside, and heavy
rain was beating against the window. The rain had been falling
like that all night, drenching a million people camped in the
streets. What should have been a rosy June morning looked
like the start of a wet, black nightmare.

Before long I was going to have to walk out into that downpour
in fancy dress because I had been too stupid to apply for a permit
to take a car up to Westminster Abbey. His Grace, the Duke of
Norfolk, Earl Marshal of England, in charge of arrangements,
had offered that choice. If I had filled out the forms, authoritative
windshield stickers would have been issued, and I could have
ridden to the Abbey in the splendor of the Dorsey Daimler.

I had laughed at the idea. An absurd fuss, a preposterous
waste of car-rental money, I told Joan. Living within a short
walk of the Abbey, I could easily stroll up there on a lovely June
morning. It wasn't just chintziness that impelled me to walk.
The American in me was tickled by the idea of walking to a coronation instead of being chauffeured by a lackey in royal Daimler
glory. Thomas Jefferson walked to the Capitol for his first inau-
guration. Let the English see how Americans did these things.

Watching the rain stream against the bedroom window made
me curse my foolishness. That short walk up to the Abbey
seemed short only because I had never walked it in pouring rain.
Actually, it was at least a mile. And in top hat, white tie, tails . . .

The earl marshal's instructions had been firm about dress.
People not entitled to wear ermine, coronet, full dress uniform,
court dress, levee dress coat with white knee breeches, kilt,

robe of rank or office, or tribal dress must wear white tie and tails, with medals. I didn't have medals. Since I didn't have a dressy suit either, I rented the full rig from Moss Bros., famous among the haberdashery-wise throughout the empire and always pronounced "Moss Bross." Knowing there would be a coronation run on Moss Bros., I went early and got a fairly decent fit. Because I'd never worn tails before, I got up a little earlier than necessary this morning against the possibility I might have a breakdown getting into the thing.

Mimi fixed a big breakfast. It was going to be a long day. I had to be in position inside the Abbey by seven-thirty and wouldn't get out until four in the afternoon. The rain let up while we were eating. Mimi got the camera and, while Kathy and Allen watched, took snapshots of Daddy wearing his coronation suit so there would be a record of this great day for them to show their grandchildren.

Whatever gods may be, they were all with me this day. The rain faded to a weak drizzle, then stopped altogether just when it was time to start for the Abbey. No, I would gamble and leave the raincoat home. Walking to the Abbey in top hat, white tie, and tails could be a great gesture only if it was done right. Wrapping up in a dirty raincoat would make it comical.

Mimi was going to Gerry Fay's house to watch the day's events on television. There weren't a lot of television sets in London yet, but Gerry's house had one, and his wife, Alice, had invited several disadvantaged families like mine to come see the show. Because it was a big day for me, as well as for the queen, I kissed Mimi and the children good-bye, said, "Wish me luck," stepped out into Lower Belgrave Street, and headed toward Victoria Station.

Not a soul in sight from Eaton Square all the way to Victoria. In thundering silence, I strolled briskly along through the heavy, wet air, getting used to the feel of the high silk hat on my head, happy to discover that it was not going to tip and fall off. In my hip pocket I had a half-pint flask of brandy to keep me awake during the long day. In my hand I carried a brown-paper bag containing two sandwiches and three or four chunks of yellow cheese. In my pockets I had a sheaf of official cards issued by the earl marshal, conveying the queen's command that policemen pass me safely through all barricades and instructing me which church entrance to use, how to conduct myself while eating during the ceremony (discreetly), and where to find toilet facilities in the Abbey.

Rounding Victoria Station, I heard the hum of a great, damp concentration of humanity and saw the broad avenue leading to

Westminster packed from curb to building line on both sides. All along the six-mile route of the coronation procession, people had spent the rain-soaked night on the sidewalks. How many there were I didn't try to guess. The papers said millions, overstating it a bit, as newspapers usually do when writing of crowds. Still, there were plenty.

I had walked among them the night before. They were bedded down in sleeping bags and soggy quilts, under raincoats, and makeshift oilskin tents. Many had brought camp stools, portable stoves, knapsacks, picnic baskets, knitting bags, radios. They brewed tea on the sidewalk, they read, they slept, they sang, they sat stoically in the rain with only a felt hat against the downpour, they dozed with heads pillowed against tree trunks and lamppost standards.

During the war Londoners' ability to "take it," no matter how much punishment the Luftwaffe gave them, became such a cliché that it later turned into a small joke. On this cold, bitter, rainy night, with those good-natured hordes cheerfully camped on rainswept concrete, I had a glimpse of that peculiar British fortitude, dogged and indomitable in the face of adversity, which made them so formidable to Hitler.

At the morning's soggy dawn, in my top hat and tails and graced, I hoped, with some of the elegance Fred Astaire brought to the uniform, I presented my credentials to the police guarding the barricades on the route to the Abbey. Miracle of miracles! The police recognized them, passed me through, waved me into the broad empty avenue called Victoria, flanked on both sides by thousands waiting for a glimpse of history. The avenue ran straight to Westminster Abbey. I prayed I could make it before the skies opened again and stepped out as rapidly as I could without losing dignity before the damp mob staring at me.

And, yes, now applauding me. A smattering of applause came off the sidewalks as I strode along. They had been waiting so long for something wonderful to appear. Now here was the first sign that wonders would indeed pass before their eyes this day. I fancied myself a vision for them out of a Fred Astaire movie, a suave, graceful gentleman in top hat, white tie, and tails, signaling the start of a momentous event.

Not a vehicle moved from one end of Victoria to the other. It had been completely cleared to await the procession. At that moment, I was the procession. The applause grew as I stepped along. Having always prided myself on shyness, modesty, and distaste for theatrics, I was surprised to find I was not only enjoying my big moment, but also, here and there where the applause seemed especially enthusiastic, tipping my silk hat to the audience.

It wasn't until I got within a block or two of the Abbey that I understood what was truly happening. There I noticed a man in the crowd talking to a companion and pointing to my hand that held the brown bag with my lunch. At this, his companion laughed, then applauded vigorously, and the light broke upon me. What delighted the crowd was the spectacle of a toff, a regular toff as I must have looked to them, brown-bagging his lunch to the coronation.

By this time I was certain to reach the Abbey before the downpour resumed. That certainty and the pleasure of strutting a great stage exhilarated me. Triumphantly, I raised my lunch over my head and waved it at the crowd, and was washed with a thunder of cheering and applause that the great Astaire himself might have envied.

That was the high point of the day for me. A moment later I passed into the Abbey and a long day's work.

Except for the coronation, I probably would never have got to London. The coronation was what the trade called a color story, and I had made a reputation in Baltimore for being a good color writer. It was a curse in some ways because writing color meant getting stuck with the dreariness of covering parades, the annual arrival of the circus, and the hubbub surrounding events like the Preakness. These stories soaked up a lot of adjectives because they never produced any news that could be told in lean, exciting verbs. It was fun to do them at first because of the garish writing that was permitted. Since they were always the same year after year, however, a long diet of them led to boredom, then softening of the brain.

My reputation as a color writer should have been the end of me, but I was lucky in death and politics. In 1952 King George VI died and General Dwight Eisenhower was elected President of the United States. The timing of the king's death meant Elizabeth's coronation would take place the following June. Eisenhower's election meant the *Sun's* veteran correspondents, who would normally have covered the coronation, would be tied down in Washington reporting the beginning of a new government. The coronation might be a grand picnic, a magnificent party, but basically it was just another color story.

Well, I had also done some real news reporting in Baltimore that showed I could also write with verbs. There would be news, too, to cover in London. "Hard news," the trade called it. But the big story would be the coronation. A color story. Buck thought about a color writer who could also use verbs. Then he invited me to lunch at the Chesapeake.

Since television has come of age, spectacles like the coronation have shrunk in importance for newspapers. Television's ability to make a faraway audience feel present at these dazzling shows is incomparable. Once newspapers conceded it, they mostly gave up trying to compete. In 1953, however, television was still learning to toddle, the coronation was still an immensely important newspaper story, and newspapers made expensive efforts to beat each other in the competition. The task of a reporter was to bring it to life on a printed page, to make the reader see it with something of the same intensity that television would later produce with cameras, satellite transmission, and a thousand other technological wonders still to come.

So when I entered Westminster Abbey at 7:30 in the morning I realized that my performance this day had better be good. So far my work in London had been a hit with Dorsey. His visit in March had changed things between us in a way that made me think we were even on a friendly footing. Still, back on his home ground in Baltimore, he was more complicated than my pal Buck, international sightseer; back home, he was also Dorsey the gambling man who had a big bet riding on my performance in London. He had put me there because of the coronation. This was the day for collecting bets or tearing up the tickets.

If I was not terrified by the trials of the day, it was because of the self-confidence gained from Buck's London visit. It had been a triumph from start to finish, and I knew Buck associated me with that triumph. My wisest move had been to introduce him immediately to Gerry and Alice Fay. I guessed Gerry's wit and man-about-London poise would appeal to Buck's love for sophisticated urbanity, and I guessed the two would make good drinking companions. My judgment proved perfect. Before the week was out they had become friends for life, and the Fays had a standing invitation to Baltimore to stay with the Dorseys.

"Dorsey is an extremely easy guest to entertain," I wrote my mother. "He is a great Anglophile and pronounces himself delighted so far by everything he has seen. He's like a kid wandering through a storybook land. He was saying yesterday he doesn't think he will want to leave here for Paris."

With Gerry and Alice, we made London a weeklong party, and when Dorsey's wife, Becky, arrived on the *Queen Elizabeth*, she joined the party enthusiastically. We drank Pernod in exotic Soho joints, sampled beer in pubs from London Bridge to Chelsea, and sipped vintage Bordeaux, Burgundies, and brandy in London's best restaurants. These included one in Mayfair, where, I told my mother, "A fabulous meal for just three of us cost $40, but fortunately I wasn't paying, so that was Dorsey's worry."

I took him underground to show him the marvels of the London subway system, which left him unimpressed. "Let's get out of here," he said. "People on subways all over the world all have the same defeated look."

The stately black London cabs were more his style, especially the older models in which drivers sat exposed to the weather while passengers rode in the enclosed cushioned depths behind. In these we crisscrossed London. Coming up from Knightsbridge toward Piccadilly one day, he began saying the *Sun* should buy a house in London as a permanent residence for its correspondents.

"That's the house we ought to buy," he said as we passed Hyde Park Corner, and pointed to a handsome stone structure with a large portico.

"That's Apsley House," I said. "I don't think it would be for sale."

"Why not?"

"It was the Duke of Wellington's house," I said.

By the time the Dorseys left for Paris, matters among us rested blissfully on a comforting "Russ" and "Becky" and "Buck" foundation. Leaving London reluctantly for what he anticipated would be the horrors of France, Buck urged me to join them in Paris on the weekend. I didn't. No use pushing your luck.

I had a good seat in the Abbey. It was in the north transept looking down from about mezzanine level onto the central ceremonial theater. It provided a clear, unobstructed view of the queen and the throne in left profile. Opposite in the south transept sat the lords and ladies of the realm in scarlet and ermine. The few good seats allotted American correspondents had been distributed by a lottery drawing, and I had got lucky.

After being ushered up the ramp to the chair I was to occupy for the next seven or eight hours, I took a spiral notepad out of my pocket and began taking notes, just as I would have done at a three-alarm fire in Baltimore, or covering a liquor-store shooting or Santa Claus's arrival in the Thanksgiving Day Parade.

This was by design. After worrying for weeks how to cover a coronation, I had decided to cover it pretty much the way I would cover any routine assignment on the local staff. I would show up, keep my eyes open, listen closely, and make notes on what I saw and heard, just as though I were going to phone the story to Banker or Spry on the rewrite desk. With the coronation, of course, I would have to get back to the office and write the story myself.

My hope was to produce a story that seemed fresh, and I thought this might be possible if I treated it as though I'd just strolled into the newsroom one afternoon and Cauley had come dancing at me and shouting: "They're having a coronation up at the Abbey in ten minutes. Get up there as fast as you can."

This was not the safe way to cover the coronation, but it offered the best chance of doing a good story. The safe way was to write the story before the event was held. This was the easiest way, too. It was also the surest way to produce a lifeless story.

I considered writing the story in advance. It could easily be done. The thing was really nothing more than a pageant, an immense pageant, to be sure, but a pageant nevertheless. Every line of the script, every move in the ceremony, everything was available weeks beforehand. The plot line was as predictable as a Chinese opera. I could write the story in advance, so it would be ready to cable to Baltimore if I couldn't produce a fresh story writing on deadline after getting out of the Abbey.

This idea I discarded quickly. For one thing, I was cocky about my ability to produce a fresh story of several thousand words under deadline pressure. I had always worked well on deadlines, maybe even better than when there was time to dawdle. Also, why go through the tedium of writing the entire story ahead of time if I didn't intend to use it?

So I entered the Abbey with no backup story ready to send in case of emergency, took out my spiral pad, and started jotting notes on what I saw. Tier upon tier of dark blue seats edged with gold. The stone walls draped with royal purple and gold. The stained glass of rose windows transforming the gray outer light into streams of red, yellow, green, and blue high up against the Abbey roof.

Many of these notes were to appear almost unchanged in my story.

"A glistening African woman in a dress of glistening gold jangled the dozen dainty gold bracelets adorning her pudgy arms."

"Yellow men and tan men, black men and pink men, men with *cafe au lait* skins and men with the red veined nose of country squiredom."

"Malayans with bands of orange and brown-speckled cloth bound tightly about their hips . . ."

"Men dressed as Nelson might have dressed when he was sporting in London . . . like courtiers who dallied with the Restoration beauties of Charles II's court . . . like officers in Cornwallis's army . . ."

". . . violins far away eerily unreal . . ."

Writing to my mother later, I disposed of the coronation in a single paragraph:

"I am so sick of the whole business that I can't write about it. Suffice it to say that I was in the Abbey about seven and didn't get out until four P.M. In this time I ate two sandwiches, several chunks of cheese, went to sleep three times, and drank a half pint of brandy to keep my blood flowing. I was seated in the midst of all the African and Oriental potentates and had a fine view of the staircase leading down to the water closets, where I could see Africans in leopard skins and Chinese dressed like French admirals queuing up to wait their turn to make water. I came out of the Abbey, stiff as a board and woozey, and had to run through a cold driving rainstorm to find a taxicab. Then I had to write for six hours, producing that mass of type which ran in the *Sun*. I didn't feel that I laid an egg completely, because next day mine was the only story from any American newspaper which had parts reproduced in any of the London papers. Considering that papers like the *New York Times* and *Tribune* had twenty-five and thirty reporters to do the job, I felt we did fairly well."

The humility in this last sentence was entirely bogus. By the time I wrote my mother the reaction from Baltimore was in, and I felt I had done far better than fairly well. I felt I had scored an absolute triumph. The day following the coronation, I had a cable signed by sixteen members of the city staff, including Janetta, Banker, Caulfield, and Ed Young. It said:

MAGNIFICENT. YOUR COVERAGE WORTHY OF THE CORONATION, AND OF BAKER.

Pete Kumpa, one of the best newsmen on the staff and an old friend whose regular correspondence kept me posted on events in the home office, reported: "Your story received here in the greatest admiration. Magnificent is the word."

The greatest ego bloater of all, however, was a note from Becky Dorsey marked "Very Personal." She reported various compliments about the coronation piece that Buck had received from various high-and-mighty types in the *Sun* hierarchy, then said:

"The nicest of all—Tom O'Neill said, 'Buck, the boy knows how to use the English language. It's a finished piece, beautifully done'—"

Closing, Becky wrote, "I do not know that Buck would approve of my telling you all this, but on thinking of that fine ignorant old face of yours, I couldn't help myself."

I could have discounted praise from my friends on the city staff. They had been writing glowing reviews from my very first days in London. They were my cheering section back in Baltimore, and for good reason. Being picked from the local staff for the *Sun's* plum assignment abroad, I was a symbol of hope for them. If one man from the local staff could escape into the glorious world of foreign correspondence, there might be hope for all. They had a stake in seeing me succeed and wrote constantly, applauding and cheering me on to keep my morale high.

Becky's report about Tom O'Neill, however, was not so easily explained away. Nothing could have done more to puff me with self-admiration than those few words about Tom O'Neill's remarks to Buck. I was not the type to have wildest dreams, but if I had been, the wildest I could have concocted would have had Buck Dorsey listening with the respect he always accorded his favorite reporter as the great O'Neill heaped me with praise.

Two months after the coronation had crowned me with glory, my triumph was confirmed in a cable from Baltimore:

TEN DOLLAR MERIT RAISE EFFECTIVE NEXT WEEK FOR YOU. HAPPY AUGUST FOURTH AND ALL THAT. LOVE. DORSEY.

That brought my salary up to $120 a week. I was a $6,240-a-year man.

My Experience with ALS

by Stephen Hawking

STEPHEN W. HAWKING

Stephen W. Hawking is one of the world's great theoretical scientists, whose work explores concepts about the universe and beyond. He has lived for many years with amyotrophic lateral sclerosis (also known as "Lou Gerhig's Disease"), a degenerative illness. Mr. Hawking is confined to a wheelchair with extremely limited physical motion and speech. He is best known for his book A Brief History of Time: From the Big Bang to Black Holes, *written in 1988. It was a bestseller that explained difficult scientific concepts in a way that could be understood by a wide audience.*

I AM quite often asked: How do you feel about having ALS? The answer is, not a lot. I try to lead as normal a life as possible and not think about my condition or regret the things it prevents me from doing, which are not that many.

It was a very great shock to me to discover that I had motor neurone disease. I had never been very well coordinated physically as a child. I was not good at ball games, and maybe for this reason I didn't care much for sport or physical activities. But things seemed to change when I went to Oxford. I took up coxing and rowing. I was not Boat Race standard, but I got by at the level of intercollege competition.

In my third year at Oxford, however, I noticed that I seemed to be getting clumsier, and I fell over once or twice for no apparent reason. But it was not until I was at Cambridge, in the following year, that my mother noticed and took me to the family doctor. He referred me to a specialist, and shortly after my twenty-first birthday I went into the hospital for tests. I was in for two weeks, during which I had a wide variety of tests. They took a muscle sample from my arm, stuck electrodes into me, injected some radio-opaque fluid into my spine, and watched it going up and down with X-rays as they tilted the bed. After all that, they didn't tell me what I had, except that it was not multiple sclerosis and that I was an atypical case. I gathered, however, that they expected it to continue to get worse and that there was nothing they could do except give me vitamins. I could see that they didn't expect them to have much effect. I didn't feel like asking for more details, because they were obviously bad.

The realization that I had an incurable disease that was likely to kill me in a few years was a bit of a shock. How could something like that happen to me? Why should I be cut off like this? However, while I was in the hospital, I had seen a boy I vaguely knew die of leukemia in the bed opposite me. It had not been a pretty sight. Clearly there were people who were worse off than me. At least my condition didn't make me feel sick. Whenever I feel inclined to be sorry for myself, I remember that boy.

Not knowing what was going to happen to me or how rapidly the disease would progress, I was at a loose end. The doctors told me to go back to Cambridge and carry on with the research I had just started in general relativity and cosmology. But I was not making much progress because I didn't have much mathematical background—and anyway, I might not live long enough to finish my Ph.D. I felt somewhat of a tragic character. I took to listening to Wagner, but reports in magazine articles that I drank heavily are an exaggeration. The trouble is, once one article said it, then other articles copied it because it made a good story. Anything that has appeared in print so many times must be true.

My dreams at that time were rather disturbed. Before my condition was diagnosed, I had been very bored with life. There had not seemed to be anything worth doing. But shortly after I came out of the hospital, I dreamt that I was going to be executed. I suddenly realized that there were a lot of worthwhile things I could do if I were reprieved. Another dream that I had several times was that I would sacrifice my life to save others. After all, if I was going to die anyway, it might as well do some good.

But I didn't die. In fact, although there was a cloud hanging over my future, I found to my surprise that I was enjoying life in the present more than I had before. I began to make progress with my research. I got engaged and married, and I got a research fellowship at Caius College, Cambridge.

The fellowship at Caius took care of my immediate employment problem. I was lucky to have chosen to work in theoretical physics because that was one of the few areas in which my condition would not be a serious handicap. And I was fortunate that my scientific reputation increased at the same time that my disability got worse. This meant that people were prepared to offer me a sequence of positions in which I only had to do research without having to lecture.

We were also fortunate in housing. When we were married, Jane was still an undergraduate at Westfield College in London, so she had to go up to London during the week. This meant that we had to find somewhere I could manage on my own and that was centrally located, because I could not walk far. I asked the College if they could help, but was told by the then bursar: It is College policy not to help fellows with housing. We therefore put our name down to rent one of a group of new flats that were being built in the marketplace. (Years later, I discovered that those flats were actually owned by the College, but they didn't tell me that.) When we returned to Cambridge from the summer in America, however, we found that the flats were not ready. As a great concession, the bursar offered us a room in a hostel for graduate students. He said, "We normally charge twelve shillings and sixpence a night for this room. However, as there will be two of you in the room, we will charge twenty-five shillings."

We stayed there only three nights. Then we found a small house about one hundred yards from my university department. It belonged to another College, which had let it to one of its fellows. He had recently moved out to a house in the suburbs, and he sublet the house to us for the remaining three months on his lease. During those three months, we found another house in the same road standing empty. A neighbor summoned the owner from Dorset and told her it was a scandal that her house should be vacant when young people were looking for accommodation, so she let the house to us. After we had lived there for a few years, we wanted to buy it and do it up, so we asked my College for a mortgage. The College did a survey and decided it was not a good risk. So in the end we got a mortgage from a building society, and my parents gave us the money to do it up.

We lived there for another four years, until it became too difficult for me to manage the stairs. By this time, the College appreciated me rather more and there was a different bursar. They therefore offered us a ground-floor flat in a house that they owned. This suited me very well because it had large rooms and wide doors. It was sufficiently central that I could get to my university department or the College in my electric wheelchair. It was also nice for our three children, because it was surrounded by a garden that was looked after by the College gardeners.

Up to 1974, I was able to feed myself and get in and out of bed. Jane managed to help me and bring up two children without outside help. Thereafter, however, things became more difficult, so we took to having one of my research students living with us. In return for free accommodation and a lot of my attention, they helped me get up and go to bed. In 1980 we changed to a system of community and private nurses who came in for an hour or two in the morning and evening. This lasted until I caught pneumonia in 1985. I had to have a tracheostomy operation, and from then on I needed twenty-four-hour nursing care. This was made possible by grants from several foundations.

Before the operation my speech had been getting more slurred, so that only people who knew me well could understand me. But at least I could communicate. I wrote scientific papers by dictating to a secretary, and I gave seminars through an interpreter who repeated my words more clearly. However, the tracheostomy removed my ability to speak altogether. For a time, the only way I could communicate was to spell out words letter by letter by raising my eyebrows when someone pointed to the right letter on a spelling card. It is pretty difficult to carry on a conversation like that, let alone write a scientific paper. However, a computer expert in California named Walt Woltosz heard of my plight. He sent me a computer program he had written called Equalizer. This allowed me to select words from a series of menus on the screen by pressing a switch in my hand. The program could also be controlled by a head or eye movement. When I have built up what I want to say, I can send it to a speech synthesizer.

At first, I just ran the Equalizer program on a desktop computer. Then David Mason, of Cambridge Adaptive Communications, fitted a small personal computer and a speech synthesizer to my wheelchair. This system allows me to communicate much better than I could before. I can manage up to fifteen words a minute. I can either speak what I have written or save it on disk. I can then print it out or call it back and speak it sentence by sentence. Using this system I have written two books and a number of scientific papers. I have also given a number of scientific and popular talks. They have been well received. I think that is in a large part due to the quality of the speech synthesizer, which is made by Speech Plus. One's voice is very important. If you have a slurred voice, people are likely to treat you as mentally deficient. This synthesizer is by far the best I have heard because it varies the intonation and doesn't speak like a Dalek. The only trouble is that it gives me an American accent. However, by now I identify with its voice. I would not want to change even if I were offered a British-sounding voice. I would feel I had become a different person.

I have had motor neurone disease for practically all my adult life. Yet it has not prevented me from having a very attractive family and being successful in my work. This is thanks to the help I have received from my wife, my children, and a large number of other people and organizations. I have been lucky that my condition has progressed more slowly than is often the case. It shows that one need not lose hope.

from

Long Walk to Freedom

by Nelson Rolihlahla Mandela

ON February 2, 1990, F. W. de Klerk stood before Parliament to make the traditional opening speech and did something no other South African head of state had ever done: he truly began to dismantle the apartheid system and lay the groundwork for a democratic South Africa. In dramatic fashion, Mr. de Klerk announced the lifting of the bans on the ANC, the PAC, the South African Communist Party, and thirty-one other illegal organizations; the freeing of political prisoners incarcerated for nonviolent activities; the suspension of capital punishment; and the lifting of various restrictions imposed by the State of Emergency. "The time for negotiation has arrived," he said.

It was a breathtaking moment, for in one sweeping action he had virtually normalized the situation in South Africa. Our world had changed overnight. After forty years of persecution and banishment, the ANC was now a legal organization. I and all my comrades could no longer be arrested for being a member of the ANC, for carrying its green, yellow, and black banner, for speaking its name. For the first time in almost thirty years, my picture and my words, and those of all my banned comrades, could freely appear in South African newspapers. The international community applauded de Klerk's bold actions. Amidst all the good news, however, the ANC objected to the fact that Mr. de Klerk had not completely lifted the State of Emergency or ordered the troops out of the townships.

On February 9, seven days after Mr. de Klerk's speech opening Parliament, I was informed that I was again going to Tuynhuys. I arrived at six o'clock in the evening. I met a smiling Mr. de Klerk in his office and as we shook hands, he informed me that he was going to release me from prison the following day. Although the press in South Africa and around the world had been speculating for weeks that my release was imminent, Mr. de Klerk's announcement nevertheless came as a surprise to me. I had not been told that the reason Mr. de Klerk wanted to see me was to tell me that he was making me a free man.

I felt a conflict between my blood and my brain. I deeply wanted to leave prison as soon as I could, but to do so on such short notice would not be wise. I thanked Mr. de Klerk, and then said that at the risk of appearing ungrateful I would prefer to have a week's notice in order that my family and my organization could be prepared for my release. Simply to walk out tomorrow, I said, would cause chaos. I asked Mr. de Klerk to release me a week from that day. After waiting twenty-seven years, I could certainly wait another seven days.

De Klerk was taken aback by my response. Instead of replying, he continued to relate the plan for my release. He said that the government would fly me to Johannesburg and officially release me there. Before he went any further, I told him that I strongly objected to that. I wanted to walk out of the gates of Victor Verster and be able to thank those who looked after me and greet the people of Cape Town. Though I was from Johannesburg, Cape Town had been my home for nearly three decades. I would make my way back to Johannesburg, but when I chose to, not when the government wanted me to. "Once I am free," I said, "I will look after myself."

De Klerk was again nonplused. But this time my objections caused a reaction. He excused himself and left his office to consult with others. After ten minutes he returned with a rather long face and said, "Mr. Mandela, it is too late to change the plan now." I replied that the plan was unacceptable and that I wanted to be released a week hence and at Victor Verster, not Johannesburg. It was a tense moment and, at the time, neither of us saw any irony in a prisoner asking not to be released and his jailer attempting to release him.

De Klerk again excused himself and left the room. After ten minutes he returned with a compromise: yes, I could be released at Victor Verster, but, no, the release could not be postponed. The government had already informed the foreign press that I was to be set free tomorrow and felt they could not renege on that statement. I felt I could not argue with that. In the end, we agreed on the compromise, and Mr. de Klerk poured a tumbler of whisky for each of us to drink in celebration. I raised the glass in a toast, but only pretended to drink; such spirits are too strong for me.

I did not get back to my cottage until shortly before midnight, whereupon I immediately sent word to my colleagues in Cape Town that I was to be released the following day. I managed to get a message to Winnie and I telephoned Walter in Johannesburg. They would all fly in on a chartered plane the next day. That evening, a number of ANC people on what was known as the National Reception Committee came to the cottage to draft a statement that I would make the following day. They left in the early hours of the morning, and despite my excitement, I had no trouble falling asleep.

Icon of Hope for Burma

by Eileen Lucas

AUNG SAN SUU KYI was born June 19, 1945, in Rangoon, the capital of Burma. Since 1885, the ancient kingdom of Burma had been a British colony; that was about to end. The Burma Independence Army, led by General Aung San, fought both the Japanese and British during World War II in an effort to win independence. Just as that independence was about to be achieved, General Aung San was assassinated on July 19, 1947, by followers of a political rival. Only 32 years old when he died, he would be remembered as a hero by the Burmese people. On January 4, 1948, Burma became an independent republic.

In addition to his two-year-old daughter, Aung San left two sons, Aung San Oo and Aung San Lin, but sadly, the younger son Lin died in a drowning accident. Bravely, their mother, Daw Khin Kyi, continued the work of her husband as a member of Burma's Parliament, resigning to become director of the Children and Mothers Welfare Board. This work led her to other service positions, and offered her the opportunity to travel to other parts of Asia and the world.

Daw Khin Kyi became Burmese ambassador to India when Suu Kyi was 15. Suu Kyi happily traveled with her, and completed her schooling in India. She learned about and developed an appreciation for the principles of nonviolence taught by the great Indian leader Mohandas Gandhi. Suu Kyi worked hard and was always one of the best students in her class, but there was time for recreation too. Her mother enrolled her in riding lessons with the children of other diplomats, and the grandchildren of Indian Prime Minister Jawaharlal Nehru. Always she was reminded of her father, who had consulted with Nehru. Nearly every 19th of July, she returned to Burma with her mother for the observance of Martyr's Day, when her father and others were mourned and remembered.

In 1964, Aung San Suu Kyi traveled to England to attend St. Hugh's College, Oxford. She studied philosophy, politics, and economics, and graduated in 1967. At that time a Burmese leader, U Thant, was Secretary General of the United Nations, which probably inspired Suu Kyi to seek work there. She moved to New York City, got an apartment, and went to work as an information officer for the United Nations. In her spare time, she volunteered at Bellevue Hospital, a place for the city's poor suffering from physical and mental problems.

The years Aung San Suu Kyi spent abroad had been difficult ones for her homeland. In 1962, a military takeover led by General Ne Win resulted in a government of only one political party, Ne Win's Burmese Socialist Program Party. No opposition to that party would be allowed, as Ne Win proved in July 1962 when soldiers opened fire on students on a university campus. As Bertil Lintner reports in his book *Outrage,* "Officially, 15 were killed and 27 wounded. But both neutral observers and students who were present during the shooting say that the university looked like a slaughterhouse where not 15 but hundreds of potential leaders of society lay sprawled in death."

As Ne Win ruled Burma with a heavy hand, Suu Kyi made decisions that determined the course of her life. On January 1, 1972, she married Michael Aris, a British scholar she met at Oxford. Aris was employed in Bhutan as a private tutor to that small Himalayan country's royal family. Daw Aung San Suu Kyi ("Daw" is a title of respect for an adult woman, somewhat like "Mrs.") worked in Bhutan's Foreign Ministry, and advised the government on United Nations affairs.

The couple was very happy, but Aung San Suu Kyi foresaw that the day might come when her devotion to her homeland might make things difficult. Before their marriage, she wrote to Michael, "I only ask one thing, that should my people need me, you would help me to do my duty by them."

In 1973, they moved to Oxford, England. There they had two sons, Myint San Aung (also known as Alexander) and Htein Lin (Kim).

During the following years, Aung San Suu Kyi regularly visited Rangoon to see her mother and to do research on her father and his work. She made sure that her sons were brought up with an understanding of their Burmese heritage. She taught for a while at a university in Japan, and later continued her own studies in India. In April 1988, she had just begun work on her post graduate thesis in London, when she received word that her mother suffered a stroke. Immediately she traveled to Burma; she cared for her mother in the hospital until she was able to bring her to the family home in July, when she was joined by her husband and sons.

The spring of 1988 was an explosive time in Burma. For some months students had been demonstrating, calling for a multiparty general election. Hundreds of students had been arrested and some were killed by government forces. Students released from government detention told horrific tales of torture. Security officers wanted to pinpoint the movement's organizers. They did not believe such demonstrations could have been a spontaneous response to years of injustice. The demonstrations and government reprisals continued into the summer months. Hundreds of thousands of students, monks, and ordinary citizens marched for democracy in Rangoon and other places. According to one report, between August 8th and 12th at least 1,000 people were killed in the army's response to these marches.

Aung San Suu Kyi watched these developments with horror as she cared for her ailing mother. She had always kept her Burmese citizenship, and gradually came to realize that as her father's daughter, it was impossible for her to remain quiet any longer. On August 15 she sent a letter to the government asking that a committee be formed to deal with the crisis. When her letter was not answered, she arranged to speak at the rally on August 26. As she stood on a stage below a portrait of her father, she said that though 40 years had passed since Burma had won its independence from Britain, its people were now engaged in a "second struggle for national independence." She continued:

> A number of people are saying that since I've spent most of my life abroad and am married to a foreigner, I could not be familiar with the ramifications of this country's politics. But these facts have never, and will never interfere with or lessen my love and devotion for my country by any measure or degree. . . . People have been saying that I know nothing of Burmese politics. The trouble is, I know too much. My family knows best how complicated and tricky Burmese politics can be and how much my father had to suffer on this account.

Many who had come to hear the speech out of curiosity left convinced that they now had a leader who would fight for the restoration of democracy in their country. Many ordinary citizens were inspired to join the cause. Many members of the only political party (known as the BSPP) resigned.

Aung San Suu Kyi called for a multiparty election. Instead, on Sunday, September 18, General Saw Maung assumed power in a military takeover of the already military-influenced government.

Maung called himself the head of the State Law and Order Council (SLOC) to ensure "peace and tranquility." He said he would allow new political parties to form, but he banned political gatherings. As author Kanbawza Win reported, the military crackdown that followed was carried out "with cold-blooded efficiency. Any crowd in sight was mowed down systematically as the tanks and armored cars rumbled down in perfect formations." It was reported by witnesses that hundreds, perhaps thousands, of Burmese were killed by their own military.

The killings brought the Burmese struggle for democracy to the world's attention. "I would like every country in the world to recognize the fact that the people of Burma are being shot down for no reason at all," Aung San Suu Kyi said in a public statement. Refusing to be intimidated, she participated in the founding of an opposition political party, the National League for Democracy, on September 24, and became its first general secretary. She traveled around Burma, speaking out for democracy despite the government's ban on such activities. When she visited the town of Moulmein, the military through loudspeakers on army trucks, ordered people not to leave their houses; still they flocked to see her.

Always she reminded people that their protest must be nonviolent. "Only if we can control ourselves can we win over our enemies," she said. Author Kanbawza Win suggests, "The spectacle of tens of thousands standing in silence, listening attentively for hours on end to an entirely new message of democracy through discipline, responsibility and nonviolent struggle, must have sent cold shivers down the spine of U Ne Win and his generals."

In the midst of her campaigning, Aung San Suu Kyi saw her mother's health continue to decline. On December 27, 1988, the courageous widow of General Aung San died, and even the military government leaders had to pay their respects to Aung San Suu Kyi in her grief. The funeral on January 2 was attended by hundreds of thousands, but the day passed peacefully. Within weeks Aung San Suu Kyi resumed speaking out for democracy.

By June of 1989 she was challenging the army to end their support of the dictatorship, saying, "My father didn't build up the army in order to oppress the people." On July 20, Michael Aris, who had returned to England, heard the news that his wife had been placed under house arrest. Returning to Burma immediately, he was detained by government officials and told that he could join his wife only if he promised not to make any statements to anyone else while he was there. In other words, he,

113

too, would be under house arrest. Aris responded that he only wanted to be with his wife and their sons. When he was taken to her house, he was relieved to learn that Aung San Suu Kyi was safe, but she had begun a hunger strike to protest the arrest of many of her young supporters. She maintained her hunger strike for 12 days until she was assured that the detainees would not be harmed. On September 2, Aris and the boys returned to England. They would be allowed no contact with her for long periods of time.

It was obvious that the government hoped that cutting Aung San Suu Kyi off from her supporters would mean the end of the democracy movement. But in the 11 months since her first speech, she had made a difference in Burma. She gave the people a taste of freedom from fear. As Kanbawza Win says, "Her invisibility did not leave the Burmese uncertain of what she wanted them to do."

Though she was declared ineligible for election by the government, when the elections were held May 27, 1990, the people voted overwhelmingly for her party, the NLD. Although the military's party won only about 2 percent of the vote, they refused to give up control of the government. They continued to harass and arrest members of the NLD.

Though Aung San Suu Kyi could not speak to her family or friends, they continued to speak out for her. In July 1991, the European Parliament awarded her the Sakharov Prize for freedom of thought. Because she would not have been allowed back in to the country if she left to receive the award, she could not be present to accept it.

On October 14, 1991, it was announced that she had won the Nobel Peace Prize for her nonviolent efforts on behalf of human rights in Burma. Czech author and political leader Václav Havel, who nominated her, said, "She is an outstanding example of the power of the powerless." The award was hailed as a victory for the people of Burma, as a declaration that the world had noted their struggle against a brutal regime. Students in Rangoon staged demonstrations on her behalf, and many were arrested. The government forced the NLD to expel Aung San Suu Kyi for having received support from a foreign organization.

On December 10, 1991, dignitaries from around the world gathered in Oslo, Norway, for the awarding of the Nobel Peace Prize. Over 100 Burmese people living in various places around the world were there, but Aung San Suu Kyi, still under house arrest, was not. Her son Myint San Aung accepted the prize for her and for "all the men, women and children who . . . continue to sacrifice their well-being, their freedom, and their lives in pursuit of a democratic Burma."

Time passed and Aung San Suu Kyi remained without freedom. Often she did not have enough to eat, and was forced to sell most of her furniture to buy food. She lost weight and suffered a number of nutrition-related health problems. The house in which she was prisoner fell into disrepair and weeds and snakes took over the once-beautiful garden. In February 1993, a group of Nobel Peace Prize laureates assembled in Bangkok to call for her release. In February 1994, a member of the United States Congress visited her and delivered a letter from President Bill Clinton, expressing his support for human rights and democracy in Burma.

Finally, in July 1995, word came that she was no longer under house arrest. Was she truly free, and would conditions improve in Burma? That remained to be seen. "We're nowhere near democracy," she said. "I've been released, that's all." Shortly before a NLD Conference was to be held at Aung San Suu Kyi's home May 26, 1996, the government arrested more than 200 NLD members. The conference went on anyway, although only 18 delegates were able to attend. Some 10,000 supporters gathered outside to protest the government's action. That support, and international pressure, forced the release of some of the NLD members. It is believed that many political prisoners are being subjected to torture and other inhumane treatment. Many of Burma's minorities continue to be repressed.

On August 31, 1995, a video-recorded message from Aung San Suu Kyi opened a meeting of women's groups gathered in China for a world conference on women. "For millennia women have dedicated themselves almost exclusively to the task of nurturing, protecting, and caring for the young and the old," she said, "striving for the conditions of peace that favor life as a whole. It is time to apply in the arena of the world the wisdom and experience that women have gained."

Susan Butcher

by Bill Littlefield

FOR Susan Butcher, it was a day like any other: brutally cold, windy, and snowing hard enough so that it was impossible to see more than a few feet in front of the heavy four-wheel vehicle her sled dogs were dragging for practice. In short, as far as she was concerned, everything was perfect.

Then suddenly Butcher's lead dog went "gee" (right) when Butcher shouted "Haw!" (left), and the four-wheeler, the dogs, and Butcher plunged off a twelve-foot cliff and into a clump of alder trees.

There was, of course, no path out. The trail Butcher and the dogs had fallen from was little traveled, and she figured it might be several days before somebody happened by. She had no saw and no ax. It was only supposed to be a little training run. With pliers, a wrench, and a broken screwdriver, she chopped at the alders. She got the dogs working together, and they pulled the four-wheeler up the hill. Sometimes they'd make as little as twelve inches of progress before Butcher would have to begin hacking away with her pliers and wrench again, but five hours after they'd fallen, Butcher and her dogs were on the road back to her cabin. Butcher had learned not to leave home, even for practice, without all her tools. And she hoped her lead dog had learned that "Haw!" meant "Haw!"

On that day when she and her team fell off the trail, Susan Butcher was training herself and her dogs for the Iditarod, the annual sled dog race that covers the eleven hundred miles between Anchorage and Nome, Alaska. Over the years, Butcher's consistently excellent finishes in this most grueling of athletic events have become the stuff of legend, and some of the tales of her training runs are no less dramatic than the races themselves. In a funny way, Butcher's preparation for the Iditarod began before the race ever existed. When she finally entered it for the first time in 1978, Butcher must have felt like she'd finally discovered where she belonged.

As a little girl growing up in Cambridge, Massachusetts, Susan Butcher only knew where did *not* belong. She hated the congestion of the busy streets, the constant noise of the traffic, and the pollution all around her. She begged her parents to move to the country, or at least to let her live in a tent in the backyard. Her best friends were the dogs she kept. In first grade she wrote an essay entitled "I Hate Cities." That was the first, last, and only sentence in the paper.

When she was finally old enough to leave home, she put Cambridge behind her in favor of Colorado. When the Rockies no longer seemed sufficiently remote, she headed for Alaska. She finally settled in a town called Eureka, which you will not find on many maps. There she cobbled together four one-room cabins, a doorless outhouse, and 120 doghouses. Butcher's dogs have outnumbered the two-legged citizens of Eureka by as many as 150 to 13.

Eureka is a fine place to prepare for the Iditarod, since a chief feature of both is isolation. A pitcher who's gone to a full count on the batter with the bases loaded in the ninth inning of a tie game might feel lonely. A marathoner who has run beyond whatever certainty her training can provide and still has miles to go might feel that way, too. But the Iditarod exists primarily as a tribute to the conviction that everybody ought to be able to take care of himself or herself with the help of a dozen or so dogs, and there is perhaps no loneliness like the loneliness of someone lost and snow-blind in the middle of Alaska.

A very fast and disciplined dog team with an experienced and fortunate musher can complete the race in a little over eleven days. Some competitors take as long as three weeks, and a lot of starters, as high as 30 or 40 percent some years, quit. Leaders and losers alike spend hours and hours alone and cold in a blasted white landscape. When their dog teams are traveling up a hill, the mushers run along behind them or kick with first one numb foot, then the other. When the teams are traveling downhill, the mushers hold on for their lives and pray that the wind won't freeze their eyes shut or tear the sled from their hands, leaving them without even the company of their dogs. For as long as they can stand it, they swerve over frozen rivers, navigate through the stumps of burned-over forests by the insanely inadequate glow of a single small headlight, and hope they won't suddenly crash headlong into a bear or a moose or the dog team of some poor fool who has become completely confused and started racing back-ward on the trail.

All these obstacles appeal to Susan Butcher, who's felt since early childhood that taking heat, light, and shelter for granted was missing the point. Only when she has felt close to nature's essentials has she felt challenged. And only when she has felt challenged has she felt entirely alive.

Joe Redington invented the Iditarod in 1973. He'd always loved the wilderness, particularly the Alaskan wilderness, and he was worried that what he loved was falling into the hands of snowmobilers and settlers with satellite dishes. He scratched his head and wondered how to remind everybody of the toughness and independence that Alaska had always demanded of its residents, and he came up with a race that would require sled drivers and their dogs to brave screaming winds, blinding blizzards, hunger, lack of sleep, and a dozen other hardships that most athletes would just as soon consider only from a great distance. He called the race the Iditarod after an Alaskan ghost town bearing the name, which is an old Indian word meaning distant place.

As an incentive to take up this crazy challenge, Redington offered $50,000 to the winner of the first Iditarod, though when the race started he didn't have the money. Twenty days later, when that first race ended, Joe had the dough. He'd hustled it from various individual and corporate donors. But over the years the payoff for winning the Iditarod continued to be a little on the shaky side. Winners have sometimes had to settle for their prizes in installments, unlike all the professional baseball, basketball, and football players who are secure in their guaranteed contracts.

Joe Redington first met Susan Butcher a few years after he'd come up with the Iditarod, and right away he was sure she'd win it one day. Or he was almost sure. He proposed a sled dog trek to the summit of Alaska's Denali, also known as Mount McKinley, perhaps partly to test the mettle of this remarkable young woman who'd come to the far north in search of escape from cars, buildings, and too many people. Together with seven dogs and a sled, Butcher and Redington made the 20,320-foot climb through hundred-mile-an-hour winds and over 2,000-foot-deep crevasses. It took them forty-four days. Nobody'd mushed that route before. Nobody's done it since. When they were finished, Redington was *absolutely* sure Susan Butcher would one day win the Iditarod.

But the extent to which Ms. Butcher fulfilled his prophecy must have surprised even Redington himself. Perhaps it shouldn't have. By the time she began to pile up first-place finishes in the Iditarod and other races in the late eighties, Susan Butcher had paid her dues. She'd learned from her limping pups to line up several friends year-round to help her knit booties for race days. Run out of booties on the trail, and the ice would cut the best team's paws to hamburger. She'd learned how to recognize a potential lead dog in a litter and how to raise all the dogs in her team to have confidence in her. And perhaps most important, she'd learned that her loyalty and attention to the needs of her canine partners would sometimes be rewarded by the special gifts the dogs had to give.

Eight years before she ever won an Iditarod, Butcher was mushing perhaps her best lead dog ever, Tekla, and fourteen other huskies across a frozen river in a practice run when suddenly Tekla began pulling hard to the right. Butcher kept tugging on the team to follow the trail, but Tekla wouldn't respond. Though she'd never balked before, the dog insisted on pulling the sled off the trail to the right. Butcher finally shrugged and decided to follow Tekla's lead. A moment after she'd made that decision and left the track, the whole trail itself sank into the river. "She [Tekla] had a sixth sense that saved our lives," Butcher told Sonja Steptoe of *Sports Illustrated* years later. "That day I learned that the wilderness is their domain. The dogs know more about it than I do, and I'm better off trusting their instincts."

Of course instinct is only part of it. Courage, stamina, and a cool head help, too. In 1985, with a superb team and high expectations, Susan Butcher seemed to be on her way to winning the Iditarod for the first time. But she ran into a problem no measure of preparation or instinct could have forestalled. Veering around a sharp bend in the trail one night, she was startled to find in the beam of her headlight a full-grown female moose. The dog team hit the animal before Butcher knew the moose was there. By the time Butcher could figure out what had happened, the moose was hopelessly entangled in the harnesses that connected the dogs. In the carnage that followed, two of Butcher's dogs were kicked to death and several others were badly injured. While Butcher fought to free the remaining dogs from their harnesses, the moose stomped on her shoulder and might have killed her, too, if another musher hadn't arrived on the scene and shot the moose. Butcher and her team limped to the next checkpoint and resigned from that Iditarod in the low point of her racing career.

And then, beginning in 1986, the high points began coming in quick succession. Between 1986 and 1990, she won the Iditarod four times. The hottest selling T-shirt in the state bore the legend "Alaska: Where Men Are Men and Women Win the Iditarod." After Butcher's third win in a row in 1988, Joe Redington laughed and told a reporter, "It's getting pretty hard for a man to win anything anymore. Maybe we should start a race especially for them."

It has been suggested that the formula for winning the Iditarod involves having good dogs, a good musher, and good luck—in about equal measure. The good musher is the one who can smile into the wrath of an unexpected hundred-mile-per-hour wind, but he or she better make sure the smile is behind several layers of ski mask, because when that wind joins below-zero temperatures, a smile will freeze on the lips for hours, and maybe forever. Susan Butcher proved she could brave the most vicious weather, but by the time she started winning the Iditarod, she'd learned to prepare herself and her dogs so well that all but the most hideous storms seemed routine. She'd also learned that by working closely with her dogs every day from the hour they were born, she could build a level of trust and loyalty that her competitors could only envy. Of course, this relationship demanded a good deal from Butcher, too. In 1991, she passed up the chance to win her fifth Iditarod when she decided that a blizzard raging over the last hundred miles of the course would unreasonably endanger her team. She prolonged a rest stop, waiting for the weather to improve, and finished second that year.

Even when the blizzards hold off and the moose stay out of the way, the Iditarod demands a tremendous amount from a musher. The rules require one mandatory rest period of twenty-four hours during the race, and once having met that requirement, no serious competitor stops for more than four hours at a time. Nearly all of the four hours of each stop are taken up by feeding the dogs, melting snow so they'll have water, checking their paws for cuts or cracks, mending the harnesses, and maybe catching something to eat—hot chocolate if you're fortunate enough to be stopping at a checkpoint where somebody's cooking, melted snow if you're not.

That doesn't leave much time for sleep, so the Iditarod's exhausted competitors have been known to hallucinate on the trail. In a book entitled *Woodsong,* a musher named Gary Paulsen wrote of a fellow who appeared on his sled wearing horn-rimmed glasses, clutching a stack of important-looking papers. "He is the most boring human being I have ever met," Paulsen says in his diary-like account. "He speaks in a low voice about federal educational grants and he goes on and on until at last I yell at him to shut up. The dogs stop and look back at me and of course I am alone."

Though Susan Butcher also might well be susceptible to hallucinations, her dogs probably know her too well to be surprised by anything she could say or do. Certainly she knows them well enough to astonish her friends. "Folks ask how I can call one hundred and fifty of them by name," she says, "but it's natural. They're like children. If you had one hundred and fifty kids, you'd know all their names, wouldn't you?"

Becoming the world's most successful musher and one of the very few sled dog drivers capable of making a living at the sport has never turned Susan Butcher's head, though it has gone some way toward fulfilling her dream. "I never got into this to make a lot of money," she told an interviewer before winning her fourth Iditarod, in 1990. "But to live just the way you want, to do what you love to do. . . . How could you have any complaints?"

Still, success at the Iditarod *has* changed Susan Butcher, if only a little. Before she became a celebrity, at least by Alaskan standards, she used to go off and live alone for six months or so. No people, no running water, no nothing. Now, in deference to the fact that people want to contact her and because raising and training 150 dogs takes the sort of money only sponsors can provide, she has a phone in her cabin. She has a husband there, too. His name is David Monson, and as a matter of fact the phone was probably his idea. He serves as Susan Butcher's business manager, and he probably got pretty tired of hitching up the dogs and mushing more than twenty miles every time he had to make a call.

Which is not to suggest that David Monson is exactly a softy. He got to know his future wife when they were both unknown mushers competing in the 1981 Iditarod. Monson was struggling to climb a hill and lost control of his sled, which wound up off the trail in the brush. It was the same stretch of brush Susan Butcher had already fallen into a few minutes earlier, and while they were both working to straighten out their dog teams, a third musher also skidded off the trail and landed on them. Monson remembers it as chaos: forty-five dogs and three mushers, including a very angry and competitive woman and one guy (Monson) who didn't really have much idea what he was up to. When they all finally got back on the trail, Butcher told Monson he'd better rest his dog team, and that was the last he saw of her in the race. If it wasn't love at first sight, it was close enough for the two mushers, now partners as well as competitors.

Not all the others who tackle the Iditarod have been as comfortable with Susan Butcher's triumphs in the race as David

Monson has been. Rick Swenson, the only person to have won the race as often as Butcher has, tried for some years to get the Iditarod's organizers to adopt a handicapping system that would, in effect, penalize Butcher and other women racers for weighing less than the men who mush against them. When that didn't work, Swenson took to intimating that Butcher won only because she had a lead dog of supernatural strength and endurance, an unintentional compliment, since Butcher had raised and trained the dog. Butcher herself tends to shrug off the bitterness of the men who resent a woman's success in a sport they'd like to claim as their own. "Yes, I am a woman," she told writer Carolyn Coman in an interview for the book *Body and Soul.* "Yes, it is a victory for me to win the Iditarod. But it isn't amazing that I, a woman, did it. I did it because I am capable, and women are capable."

Being capable may never before have involved such an effort. Butcher has said on several occasions that training for the Iditarod—which involves raising, feeding, running, and training her dogs as well as keeping herself in shape—is an eleven-month proposition. Small wonder that sometimes she thinks about turning her attention exclusively to some of Alaska's shorter races—the three-, four-, or five-hundred-mile jaunts. She already knows these races well. She holds the records in most of them, just as she does for the Iditarod. So easing up a little is a pleasant possibility that occupies Susan Butcher sometimes when she thinks about a post-Iditarod future.

Unhappily, there's an unpleasant possibility that concerns her, too. She has adjusted to the modern improvements David Monson has made in their cabin, but other adjustments won't come so easily to the woman who hated the noise and pollution and hustle of Cambridge when she was a little girl. The authorities have begun to improve the roads up Susan Butcher's way, and Butcher has watched "progress" suspiciously. "In ten years we may have ten or fifteen neighbors," she was overheard to say. "If that happens, we'll be gone."

Blintzes Stuffed with Cheese

by Kathleen Krull

AS a child in the Jewish ghetto of Warsaw, Poland, Icek-Herz Zynger studied the Jewish religion all day long at *cheder* (elementary school). His family was so poor—at times starving—that sometimes his only toy was a dried palm branch, and he would play with it for days. Reading outside of school made him forget his physical discomforts, especially after he discovered the tales of Edgar Allan Poe.

But the rise of anti-Jewish feeling in Europe sometimes gave him thoughts of suicide. At age thirty-one, by then known as Isaac Bashevis Singer (Bashevis is a variation on his mother's name, Bathsheba), he came to the United States. His first wife, Runya, and their son, Israel, moved to Russia and eventually to Palestine. They all escaped the Holocaust, when most Polish Jews, including some of Singer's family and friends, were killed by Nazis during World War II. All the places Singer had known in Poland were destroyed in the war; the world of his childhood was gone.

Singer began to re-create that old world in stories. He wrote in Yiddish (a mixture of German, Russian, and Slavic, written in Hebrew letters from right to left). He typed on a rickety Yiddish-character typewriter and helped translators convert the stores into English. He wrote articles for *The Jewish Daily Forward,* a New York paper that also published installments of his stories. "I have to force myself *not* to write," he admitted.

Singer was devastated by the death of his adored older brother, Israel Joshua, a well-known writer. Yet his grief drove him to work harder, and his next book, *The Family Moskat,* was the one that brought fame.

Singer was married to his second wife, Alma, for fifty-one years. She worked for Saks Fifth Avenue department store and supported both of them until his writing started to bring in money. They divided their time between an apartment in Manhattan and a condominium in south Florida.

Singer got up every morning at eight o'clock, had cereal and a grapefruit or apple, and then sometimes went back to bed, where he wrote notes in inexpensive lined notebooks. In the afternoons he took long walks, sometimes to the *Forward* office to deliver stories or to a cafeteria to meet old friends (they called him Bashevis). He seldom watched TV or went to the movies and didn't own a phonograph (so he never heard any of the recordings made of his stories).

He owned parakeets that flew free and sometimes landed on his bald head, and his neighbors knew him as someone who kept the pigeons well fed. He stopped eating meat out of his concern for animals. He wasn't a strict vegetarian, though; he ate eggs and did love blintzes stuffed with cheese.

Though he was still unknown at age forty, Singer eventually became famous and wealthy. But even then he lived simply; he was eating in a neighborhood drugstore when he learned he had won the Nobel Prize in literature. On the plane to receive his award, he read about himself in *People* magazine.

Pale and bald, Singer was the first to say he resembled an imp from one of his own stories. He wore dark suits, white shirts, and plain ties. He seemed frail, but he moved with the speed of a chipmunk. To entertain children, he was known to run around the house barking like a dog.

He died at age eighty-seven after a stroke.

from

Challengers: The Inspiring Life Stories of the Seven Brave Astronauts of Shuttle Mission 51-L

by The Washington Post

CONCORD High is a large brick building whose main entrance is framed by stone pillars. The social-studies teachers began their day at small desks in a large, brightly lit corner office on the second floor where pictures of Christopher Columbus, Albert Einstein and President Reagan hang on the walls. There is a globe, a book of maps, a stack of newspapers, an assortment of textbooks on desks and floor. The teachers check in at 7:30 A.M. and hurriedly organize their papers and lessons, until the 7:55 A.M. bell signals the start of the first class.

Down the carpeted hall, past long rows of beige lockers, is Room 305 where Christa McAuliffe taught most of her classes. There are tables instead of desks, and above the blackboard is McAuliffe's standard classroom decoration—covers from *Time* magazine. Her standard teaching tool remained the field trip. McAuliffe took her students on so many field trips—to the police station, the courts, the prisons—that other faculty members complained that her students were missing too many other classes.

She brought in speakers—members of congress, lawyers, judges, and suggested setting up an independent study program at the local court. She assigned students to watch the stock market or dress up in period costumes or keep journals like historians. School Principal Charles Foley considered McAuliffe one of the best teachers at Concord High School, and so did her peers. After observing one of McAuliffe's classes, Foley had no recommendations, no criticisms to offer: "It's reassuring for me as principal to watch a first-class teacher at work," he wrote in his evaluation.

For a teacher who liked to learn by doing and taught the same way, NASA's teacher-in-space program was an irresistible adventure. "In her mind, there was no way that she could let that go by," said Eileen O'Hara, her friend and colleague who taught for McAuliffe while she trained for the shuttle flight. As was her style, McAuliffe waited until the last minute to complete the eleven-page application.

More than 11,000 teachers applied, seventy-nine of them from New Hampshire. In April 1985, McAuliffe and Robert Veilleux, an astronomy and biology teacher from Manchester, were selected as the state's two finalists. "I'm not naive enough to think that I am the best in my profession," she told a reporter later. "I happen to be from a small state that didn't have as many applicants as California, for example. There is a lot of luck in being at the right place at the right time," she said. She told Eileen O'Hara that her goal was just to make it to Houston, as a finalist.

In essay questions on the application, McAuliffe plainly described why she wanted to be "the first U.S. private citizen in space."

"As a woman, I have been envious of those men who could participate in the space program and who were encouraged to excel in areas of math and science," she wrote. "I felt that women had indeed been left outside of one of the most exciting careers available. When Sally Ride and other women began to train as astronauts, I could look among my students and see ahead of them an ever-increasing list of opportunities.

"I cannot join the space program and restart my life as an astronaut, but this opportunity to connect my abilities as an educator with my interests in history and space is a unique opportunity to fulfill my early fantasies. I watched the Space Age being born, and I would like to participate," she said.

McAuliffe's proposal for a special space shuttle project had an appealing simplicity: a space journal, an ordinary person's chronicle of a new frontier like the diaries kept by America's earlier pioneers. "My journal would be a trilogy," she wrote. "I would like to begin it at the point of selection through the training for the program. The second part would cover the actual flight. Part three would cover my thoughts and reactions after my return.

"My perceptions as a non-astronaut would help complete and humanize the technology of the Space Age. Future historians would use my eyewitness accounts to help their studies of the impact of the Space Age on the general population."

McAuliffe—who was about to become the subject of an extraordinary number of photographs and film clips—proposed to NASA that she record her daily activity aboard the orbiter on videotape and slides. She knew that her students were always hungry to *see*. "A visual message would have a greater impact on an American public than just the written word," she wrote.

By late June 1985, McAuliffe and 112 other teachers were in Washington for interviews. Besides four former astronauts, the judges included actress Pam Dawber who had appeared in "Mork and Mindy," a television show about a man from outer space; former pro basketball player Wes Unseld; Robert Jarvik, the inventor of an artificial heart, and the presidents of three major universities.

On the teachers' first day in Washington, there was a discussion of the risks involved in a shuttle mission. Alan Ladwig, manager of NASA's spaceflight participant program, described the six million pounds of thrust needed to lift *Challenger* off the launch pad and the highly volatile chemicals used to produce that thrust. David R. Zahren, a Maryland teacher, recalled that it was like reading the warning label on a bottle of oven-cleaner: You read the warning and used it anyway, believing that nothing would happen.

By July 1, McAuliffe and nine other finalists were on their way to Houston. At the Johnson Space Center there, they were given medical and psychological tests and had a brief taste of weightlessness aboard a NASA KC135, known as "the vomit comet." On July 12, McAuliffe and the other finalists watched in an observation room behind Mission Control when a *Challenger* flight was aborted by a valve failure three seconds before blast-off. Ladwig turned to the teachers and reminded them of the risks. He asked if anyone wanted to withdraw from the competition, and they all said no. Ladwig said Scobee also met with the ten finalists and talked at length about the dangers involved. "He didn't want to give anybody the illusion that they were on any kind of joyride," Ladwig said.

When Vice-President George Bush announced a week later in Washington that Christa McAuliffe was NASA's unanimous choice to be the first teacher in space, her competitors were not surprised. McAuliffe was personable and spunky and enthusiastic. She handled the press with unstudied aplomb. Americans would be able to see themselves in her and like what they saw.

The media blitz was under way, and McAuliffe accepted it as

part of the deal. McAuliffe was whisked around the city in taxi-cabs from one television interview to another, from "ABC World News Tonight" to the "MacNeil/Lehrer NewsHour." During an interview with "Cable News Network," she told a reporter that she was not afraid. "I really see the shuttle as a safe program," she said.

Back home in Concord, McAuliffe's friends and neighbors were overjoyed. Her selection came during "Old-Fashioned Bargain Days"—three days when Main Street is closed to traffic and shopkeepers sell their goods on the sidewalks—and the announcement fueled an already festive atmosphere. A local disc jockey, already broadcasting live from a stage on Main Street, interviewed shoppers for their reaction to the news that one of Concord's own would make history.

The next day, there was McAuliffe, riding in the Lions Club Soccer Parade, sitting up on the back of a convertible with Caroline and Scott on either side of her. She wore NASA's cobalt-blue jumpsuit and a red, white and blue cap with a picture of the space shuttle on it. She was smiling from ear to ear and flashing the thumbs-up sign.

"Atta girl, Christa!" her new fans shouted from the parade route. "Go for it!"

Steve McAuliffe bought a video camera and began amassing a library of tape, even photographing the press photographing her. Christa went to Los Angeles and appeared on the "Tonight Show" with Johnny Carson, where the band played the Air Force anthem: "Off we go into the wild blue yonder . . . " In August, at a band concert on the statehouse plaza in Concord, the mayor declared Christa McAuliffe Day and gave her a tiny Concord flag—the city has no key—and a pewter plate from the governor. She conducted the band in "Stars and Stripes Forever," as the crowd clapped along.

Christa traveled to Washington later that month to begin preparation of the two "live lessons" she would teach from the shuttle. The Public Broadcasting Service would carry the lessons by satellite, and schools with satellite dishes could arrange through NASA and a project called "Classroom Earth" to receive daily transmissions from Challenger. During the first lesson, which she called "The Ultimate Field Trip," McAuliffe planned to conduct a tour of the flight deck, the shuttle controls, computers and the payload bay area. On the middeck, where McAuliffe would sit with Onizuka and Jarvis during blastoff, she planned to show her students what NASA literature called "the kinds of equipment and processes which help human beings live comfortably and safely in the microgravity environment of the shuttle." In other words, McAuliffe planned to explain how astronauts sleep, eat, dress, brush their teeth—even how the toilets work.

In the second lesson, called "Where We've Been, Where We're Going and Why" McAuliffe planned to use models of the Wright Brothers plane and a space station to discuss why the United States is exploring space.

McAuliffe also planned to conduct several experiments while she was on the shuttle including growing beansprouts and dropping Alka Seltzer in water to watch the effects of weight-lessness on effervescence. She also planned to take along a screwdriver, a toy car and a billiard ball for other experiments that would be filmed in the flight, narrated by McAuliffe on her return and distributed as educational films.

In September, McAuliffe left Concord to begin training with the shuttle crew at the Johnson Space Center. She worried that the "regular" astronauts would think she was thumbing a ride, that they would resent her. She wanted to be accepted and set out to do that in one important way: she would not pretend to be an astronaut. She wanted no special treatment. She would learn to take care of herself. She knew how to measure up. She also knew that she was not burdened with the professional pressures faced by the other six crew members, whose lives and careers were in space. When this adventure was done, McAuliffe intended to go home to Concord and teach.

Houston was hot and humid when McAuliffe moved into a furnished one-bedroom apartment off NASA Road 1 in an adult community called Peachtree Lane where NASA had previously rented apartments for private contractors in the space program. Peachtree Lane became home for eighteen weeks for McAuliffe and her understudy, Barbara Morgan, a second-grade teacher from McCall, Idaho. The two women were next-door neighbors on the second floor. Morgan's husband, Clay, a writer, was there for much of the training period, and Greg Jarvis lived in the same complex.

There could be no comparison between the rich New Hamp-shire countryside in autumn and the dull, flat land of Houston in any season. McAuliffe's apartment—a bedroom, a living room, a galley kitchen and a dining room that she converted to a study—overlooked a small grassy area with a grill, a picnic table, a pool and a jacuzzi. The heat and dampness made her so homesick that by November she had taken to setting the air conditioner in her apartment low enough so she could wear a sweater and jeans.

But the toughest adjustment was the separation from her family. She had brought some momentoes from home, including family pictures. Steve often sent samples of the childrens' school work, which hung on the walls. "While Christa Trains, Steve Plays 'Mr. Mom'" one New Hampshire headline said. The article described how Steve, accustomed to long hours in his law office, had mastered the rudiments of microwave cooking. Christa called home almost every night. She missed the parental ritual of tucking the children into their beds. She worried about finding time to hem the curtains she had sewn for the family's new playroom. But the couple felt the separation was worth it.

"You know, you're talking about a human being free of the bounds of gravity orbiting the earth," Steve told a reporter. "There aren't very many human beings that have done that. So I think most of us feel that whatever the price in terms of readjustments, of my taking on things that I probably should have been doing before and hadn't done, whatever those prices are they certainly pale in comparison to the opportunity."

"It's hard being away from home," Christa wrote to a former teacher in October, "but we realized it was a tradeoff for a chance in a lifetime."

In training, McAuliffe never lost that gee-whiz attitude, saying over and over that she couldn't believe NASA was going to let her go up in the space shuttle. But there she was, leaving the crew quarters one day, striding behind Ellison Onizuka, arms swinging as she flashed a gaping, excited smile. "It's just such an exciting experience," she said once. "I still can't believe I'm really here."

McAuliffe was a different breed from the other women—driven, professional scientists, who had made space their life's work. She remained mindful that she was not an astronaut but a "flight participant," not a technician but a teacher, a communicator. She chose her words carefully and enunciated each one precisely, at a fast clip and sometimes with a teacher's sing song. She spoke in crisp, complete sentences.

"Good morning, this is Christa McAuliffe, live from the *Challenger* and I'm going to be taking you on a field trip," she recited during a rehearsal for her televised lessons. "I'm going to start out introducing you to two very important members of the crew.

The first one is Commander Scobee, who is sitting to my left, and the second one is Michael Smith . . ."

The publicity abated while McAuliffe trained, a reprieve she must have welcomed. NASA limited interviews to two hours or less a week. McAuliffe's apartment was always off limits, as were telephone calls after hours. Along with her shuttle skills, she quickly learned some of the lessons of celebrity. She learned that she did not have to rush to every interview, because without her there was no interview, that not every autograph seeker planned to hang her portrait above the mantlepiece—some autographs were being sold instead. Critics of the Teacher in Space program said that McAuliffe was a public relations pawn, that she was being used by the Reagan administration to gain favor with teachers and by NASA to gain favor for the space program. McAuliffe believed she was improving the public's perception of teachers and enhancing the public's interest—especially children's interest—in the space program.

As the novelty of her selection wore off and her training wore on, the media's interest in McAuliffe dimmed—except at *The Concord Monitor.*

The Monitor has a small staff, thirteen reporters and a handful of editors, and a small circulation, about 21,000 readers. Publisher George Wilson is a tall, aristocratic-looking man who has lived in Concord with his family for twenty-four years. Editor Mike Pride had just returned to the *Monitor* from a Neiman journalism fellowship at Harvard University when NASA picked McAuliffe, and he and Wilson knew that this would be a very big story for a small town.

They assigned Bob Hohler, a sports writer who had recently joined the news staff, to cover McAuliffe full time, and they decided to publish two special supplements. One, "Christa's Challenge," was written for junior high school students. The other had two sections, "A Teacher in Training" and "The *Challenger's* Countdown." In the end, the newspaper's work provided a painfully detailed account of an extraordinary period of space history.

"Christa's Challenge" produced a wealth of facts about spaceflight, from rescue procedures (the astronauts would be transferred from a disabled shuttle in space to another vehicle in a thirty-four-inch-wide cloth ball with its own air supply) to cuisine (astronauts pick their menu after sampling a hundred foods, forty-five drinks and condiments before the flight). There was also a feature called "Kids Ask Christa":

Q: What do you like least about your training?

A: There's nothing that I don't like. Everything is new and fun, and remember that I'm getting ready for the ride of a life-time!"

She would tell her own students that she was reaching for the stars—and so should they.

From Houston, Hohler wrote extensively about her training, much of it focusing on what to do in an emergency. After her se-lection, McAuliffe's life-insurance premium rose so dramatically that she canceled the policy. Later, she accepted a gift of one mil-lion dollars in coverage from a Washington, D.C.-based company.

Much of McAuliffe's training involved studying workbooks on such things as how to get in and out of the shuttle, how to cook, how to use the bathroom, how to operate cameras. The books also showed her which of the shuttle's 1,300 switches to avoid.

"Frankly, we want to teach her how to stay out of the way," NASA's flight training director Frank Hughes told Hohler. When McAuliffe passed a test after each workbook, she was rewarded with a flight in a T-38 supersonic jet or a session in the huge shuttle simulator or another session of weightlessness. It was the T-38 that gave McAuliffe her greatest thrill. In a gleeful tele-phone conversation with her friend Eileen O'Hara, McAuliffe de-scribed how Scobee had once let her take control of the machine for some dives and rolls. O'Hara said Scobee was the only crew member McAuliffe mentioned to her. He and his wife June, a teacher, had adopted her, McAuliffe said, and tried to make her feel at home.

McAuliffe made notes for her "pre-mission" journal which were scattered around her apartment or dictated into a tape recorder. "I've got notes spread all over the place," she told friends. During the flight, she planned to record her observa-tions on a dictation machine small enough to fit in the palm of her hand, a technique used by astronauts on previous shuttle missions.

During breaks from training and homework, McAuliffe would page through *Good Housekeeping* magazine or work on her needlepoint. She liked to browse through a greeting card store near her apartment in Houston. Once she baked pies for the shuttle crew with fresh MacIntosh apples that she and her chil-dren had picked in a New Hampshire orchard. When they had the time, McAuliffe and Morgan went to the movies or roamed through the Armand Bayou, a nature preserve near the space center. McAuliffe played volleyball in a space center league.

Life at Peachtree Lane sometimes had the makeshift qualities of a college dormitory. When McAuliffe, Morgan and their public relations manager, Linda Long, were preparing dinner for a *New York Times* reporter and photographer, they had to hunt around for the right baking pan for shrimp and a bowl for the Caesar salad. McAuliffe and Morgan bought an ironing board that they shared with Long, who let them use the washer and dryer in her apartment. Jarvis occasionally visited for a glass of wine and talk about family and friends.

In November, Steve and the children visited (Caroline said the most exciting part of the trip for her was eating tuna fish in the NASA cafeteria). McAuliffe missed them and was sometimes weary, but she saw her odyssey in the space program as a single year of her family's life. She made clear that when her post-flight commitments to NASA were completed, she intended to return to Concord and her classroom. Meanwhile, plans for her homecoming there had gone somewhat awry.

The trouble began in December when *The Monitor* reported in a front page story that the city government had set aside $26,700 to plan an "Olympic size" celebration for McAuliffe in early March and later criticized the plans in an editorial headlined "Hype-hype-hooray." McAuliffe made clear through intermediaries that she did not want money, especially taxpayers' money, spent on a homecoming. Embarrassed officials of the Christa McAuliffe Homecoming Committee withdrew their request for the money and scaled back the plans to a small parade, a speech to the legislature and maybe a service-club luncheon.

Meanwhile, a network of neighbors continued to help Steve McAuliffe care for his children while Christa was in Houston, occasionally bringing them meals or even taking Caroline out to buy a needed pair of shoes. He joked that he knew how Prince Phillip felt, playing second fiddle to the queen, and that he had reinvented the Snickers candy bars as a breakfast food. But he knew the real value of his time alone with his children.

"I was one of those fathers who always came home after the kids were in bed," he told *The Monitor.* "I've really been surprised at how I have gotten to know them in a different way. . . .

"This is tough, really hard," he said. "I was really frantic for the first few months, but now I'm starting to get pretty comfortable. When it comes down to it, it's good to know you can make it on your own if you have to."

In a letter to Sister Mary Denisita, Christa wrote that Steve was doing "a super job" taking care of Scott and Caroline.

"He's getting to know his children better," she said, "and they are delighted to have Daddy's attention. It's going to be a wonderful year for all of us."

from
Frida Kahlo: Portrait of a Mexican Painter

by Bárbara C. Cruz

ALTHOUGH many people think that Kahlo's life was always filled with sadness and pain, many of Frida's friends "remember her as greatly enjoying life, happy, clever, and lively, always ready for fun." She celebrated all sorts of holidays, birthdays, baptisms, and saints' days. In Mexico, there are many days associated with a Catholic saint. For example, January 17 is a day celebrating St. Anthony, who is known for his love of pets and animals. December 12 is the day of Mexico's patron saint, the Virgin of Guadalupe. On each of these days, special celebrations are held, and even though Kahlo was not religious, she used every chance she had to have a party.

Kahlo loved jokes, exaggerating stories, and funny words. She made fun of herself as well as other people. Kahlo gave people nicknames that made them laugh. She called Rivera's driver "General Confusion" because things would not go right when he was involved. She teased one of the workers in the house, Manuel, by calling him "Manuel the Restless" because he was so lazy.

In addition to painting, Kahlo spent her days doing many different things. She wrote in her diary, including poems and watercolor drawings. Some afternoons she went to the movies. Other times, she went to Garibaldi Plaza where the *mariachi* bands would gather. The mariachi bands would be dressed in fancy costumes with huge *sombreros* (hats) and would sing Kahlo's favorite songs for a few *pesos* (coins).

Kahlo herself liked to sing, and many evenings were spent at La Casa Azul singing *corridos* (traditional Mexican songs) with friends. She and Rivera also had fun playing games like *cadavre exquis* (exquisite corpses). In this game, the first person draws a head and folds the paper down so that the next person cannot see it. The second person then draws the next section of the body and folds the paper down again. This continues until the entire body is drawn. When the paper is unfolded, the result is usually very funny. When Kahlo played, she used her wild imagination to create some hilarious monsters.

Kahlo decorated Casa Azul with many items from the time before the Europeans arrived in Mexico. She and Rivera also collected folk art from many different regions of Mexico. The kitchen was decorated with blue, white, and yellow tiles as were many traditional Mexican kitchens. Beautiful clay pots and wooden spoons sat on the counters. On one wall, Kahlo hung many tiny clay cups so that they spelled out "Frida" and "Diego."

Inside and outside Casa Azul were large, brightly decorated Judas figures. According to the Bible, Judas was the disciple who betrayed Jesus. These figures are found everywhere in Mexico during Easter. On the Saturday before Easter Sunday (the day Christians celebrate Jesus' resurrection), ugly, colorful figures of Judas are hung up high after being filled or tied with firecrackers. Churches ring their bells at 10:00 A.M. on Holy Saturday, giving the signal to light the firecracker Judas. The Judas figures can be seen in some of Kahlo's paintings.

Kahlo owned more than five hundred *retablos* or *ex-votos*, small paintings done on tin, thanking God or a saint for a miracle. Many Catholic churches in Mexico are filled with these paintings. Each retablo is about the size of a postcard. A retablo usually has three parts. At the top is the saint, the Virgin Mary, or God who brought about the miracle. In the center is a vivid drawing of the illness or disaster. Then at the bottom is a written description of what happened and a thank-you to the heavenly figure. Kahlo used some parts of this popular form of art in her own paintings. The painting which is most like a retablo is "Marxism Will Give Health to the Sick" (1954).

Kahlo also kept a beautiful garden full of colorful flowers and a large collection of animals. She had songbirds and parakeets, cats and dogs, monkeys, two turkeys, an eagle, and a deer as pets. One of her and Rivera's favorites was a spider monkey named Fulang Chang (meaning "any old monkey"). They allowed the pets inside the house and many of their friends remember sharing their meals with monkeys and parrots at the dining table. Another one of Kahlo's favorites, Bonito the parrot, made guests laugh by making his way through the clay pots and plates on the table to get to the butter, his favorite snack.

Every morning, Kahlo took time to choose what clothes and jewelry she was going to wear. She especially liked the clothes from Tehuantepec in Southern Mexico. These traditional dresses have bright colors, long flowing skirts, and are very festive. The Tehuana women are known for their personal strength, beauty, and independence. According to Mexican legend, Tehuana women are the ones who run the markets, take care of the money, and control the men.

Kahlo had a very special style of dress. While she was in Paris in 1939, the fashion designer Elsa Schiaparelli saw her in her beautiful Mexican clothing and created a dress in her name, *robe Madame Rivera*. Kahlo's style was even featured in *Vogue* magazine at the time. Her hand, complete with rings, was on the front cover. However, many Mexican women and men did not like her style of dress. This was a time in Mexico when people dressed in very Western styles (modern clothes like those worn in the United States and Europe). In 1948, a twenty-one-year-old bank worker said that "stylish people in Mexico think a rebozo [shawl] is the badge of a housemaid." Still, Kahlo chose to wear her beautiful traditional Mexican clothing.

Because many of Kahlo's teeth were rotted and black, she often covered her mouth when she laughed. Some people feel that this is why she rarely smiled in photographs. For special occasions, Kahlo capped her teeth with gold and diamonds. One of her friends, Parker Lesley, remembers one evening at the Palace of Fine Arts:

> No one paid any attention to the dance performance . . . Everyone stared at Frida, who wore her Tehuana dress and all Diego's gold jewelry, and clanked like a knight in armor . . . She had two gold incisors [teeth] and when she was all gussied [dressed] up she would take off the plain gold caps and put on gold caps with rose diamonds in front, so that her smile really sparkled.

Every morning, Kahlo took the time to comb, braid, and arrange her long, dark hair. Sometimes she wove brightly colored yarn through the braids. Other times she decorated her hair with flowers from her garden or with small combs she would buy at the market.

No outfit of Kahlo would be complete without a rebozo. Her rebozo was usually made out of silk or linen and Kahlo always chose a color that went well with the rest of her clothes. Her favorite rebozo was bright pink and handmade in Oaxaca, a city in southern Mexico.

Friends and family remember the wonderful parties and meals that Kahlo prepared. Not only were the foods delicious, but Kahlo also made sure that the table was beautifully set with colorful Mexican dishes, glasses, and flowers. Because Kahlo celebrated so many different holidays, there was always an excuse to throw a party. One of Kahlo's favorite times of the year was Christmas. Each year at Christmas time, Kahlo arranged a *posada* (a party that is held in Mexico at Christmas).

In Mexico, the Christmas season starts on December 16. During the nine days leading up to December 24, the posadas re-enact the story of Mary and Joseph trying to find lodging. People take the roles of Mary and Joseph and walk from house to house singing "I am tired. I beg for rest." Those inside sing back "Go away, go away, there is no room." After they are finally allowed in, a big fiesta takes place. Sweet drinks and delicious foods are served. Piñatas filled with candy and small toys are broken open. Kahlo's posadas were some of the best in Coyoacán.

To show her strong pride in her *mexicanidad,* Kahlo also celebrated many national or patriotic holidays. On March 21, Kahlo would celebrate Benito Juárez's birthday. Benito Juárez was a very popular president of Mexico from 1861 to 1872. He was the first native Mexican to hold such an important position. Juárez was known for his fight against the all-controlling power of the Catholic Church. He was especially admired for the many positive changes he brought to Mexico's poor.

September 16 is Independence Day in Mexico, marking Mexico's liberation from Spanish rule. At the beginning of the month, Kahlo would start buying small Mexican flags at the market. She would stick these little red, white, and green flags into fruits and plants all over the house as decorations. One of her favorite dishes during the national holiday was "national flag rice"—she would arrange white rice with rice colored red with tomatoes and rice stained green with chiles and herbs. She would serve this with colored drinks—green lime water, white rice water, and red Jamaica water (made with hibiscus flowers). Kahlo's guests were very delighted with her delicious patriotic food.

Even though much of Kahlo's life was painful, she also enjoyed life very much. Despite her physical and emotional hardships, she found the beautiful and the joyous things that life offered.

from It's Always Something

by Gilda Radner

AT one of our regular weekly sessions at my house, Joanna was listening to me drone on about my feelings of isolation, my anger, my hair loss, when she suddenly said, "Everything you're saying I've heard before."

"Am I boring you?" I said defensively.

"No, I just want you to know you are not alone, that other people are going through this. I wish you could have been at this meeting the other night at The Wellness Community. There was a bunch of ladies with no hair, and they were talking about it, talking about how they would take off their wigs and take off their scarves and walk proudly on the beach in Santa Monica, brave warriors battling cancer. I wish you could have been there."

Joanna had brought me literature on The Wellness Community, where she worked, and their newsletter, so I had read about their activities. They have something they call joke fests—meetings where everyone comes with a joke, just because they know laughing is good for you. I read everything she brought me. But I was afraid to be around people who had cancer, I guess because I wanted to pretend that I didn't have it. And I didn't want to get depressed, more depressed than I already was, something that I was sure would happen if I went to The Wellness Community. I was in conflict about this for a couple of months. Even Grace and Gene said, "Maybe you shouldn't go. Why upset yourself? We know how emotional you are and how you sponge up other people's problems—you probably shouldn't go."

Even my psychiatrist said, "You probably shouldn't go. You probably will get upset."

But I was curious. Every time I saw Joanna I'd ask her about The Wellness Community. What were the events that week? What did it look like? Where exactly was it in Santa Monica? Where do you park? Do you need quarters for the meters? Joanna was encouraging me to come to a sharing group that met every Friday between 11:000 A.M and 1:00 P.M. Anyone could come on a drop-in basis to share their present experiences with cancer and hear what The Wellness Community had to offer.

In January 1987, after I was over the nausea days of chemo number three, I asked Jodi if she would drive me to The Wellness Community. It was about a half hour from my house. I was so nervous that I would park in the wrong place or I wouldn't be able to find the building or I would be late. I think what I was really nervous about was what this community of cancer patients would be. Jodi and I found the parking lot easily. We were half hour early, but we went inside. We were the first ones there.

It was a cute little yellow house with a plaque on the front that said, "The Wellness Community." We walked into what looked like a living room in anybody's home. There were two women there with pink sweatshirts on that said "The Wellness Community" and big buttons that said :VICTOR" on them. There was a sweet woman named Joyce who gave us flyers and information and made us comfortable. There were three couches and a rug on the floor and phones ringing in other rooms. There was the cozy smell of food because lunch was being made for us in the kitchen. The chairs were set up in a circle in the main room. Jodi and I sat down, and on a clipboard I signed my name and address and phone number. The form asked what kind of cancer you had or whether your were there as a support person or family member. I wrote my name in an absolutely unreadable scrawling handwriting—and under "Type of Cancer" I printed neatly, "Ovarian."

At about quarter to eleven more people started to come in—all different types of people. They were mostly couples, young and old mixed together. You didn't know who had cancer and who didn't. There was a woman and her daughter. The woman was recently out of surgery and the eighteen-year-old daughter was holding her mother as if she was a little girl. This was their first time at The Wellness Community too. There were lots of women, more women than men. Most of the men came by themselves. One was a real dapper-looking guy in a maroon sport coat and gray pants. There wasn't the feeling that these were sick people, just a lot of different kinds of people, all different socioeconomic levels and ages.

At about ten after eleven the room was pretty much filled with maybe forty people. The two group leaders, Flo and Betty, both eleven-year survivors of cancer (Betty of an advance case of lymphoma and Flo of a double mastectomy), told their stories of cancer. They explained what The Wellness Community was and what it had to offer every person there. Amazingly, everything was free. There were group therapy sessions that met for two hours a week, available at many different times during the week, called "participant groups." These groups were the only Wellness Community activities that required a commitment. They were facilitated by licensed therapists. Everything else was on a drop-in basis, including instruction in guided imagery and visualization and relaxation three nights a week (like what I had learned from Joanna). There were group sessions for spouses or family members of cancer patients, nutrition and cooking discussions, lectures by doctors—oncologist and psychiatrists—workshops on anger management, potluck dinners and parties, therapy through painting, vocalizing, improvising—all techniques that would help in stress management and improve the quality of someone's life.

I learned why people go to AA meetings or Overeaters Anonymous or other self-help groups, and love them and say, "I have to get back there." If indeed God created the world and then left us on our own to work things out, then getting together with other people to communicate is what we should be doing. I learned at The Wellness Community that that is the most magic thing we have, our ability to open our mouths and communicate with each other.

There was a beautiful woman at the meeting, dressed perfectly in fashion. She said she had breast cancer that had metastazied and was now in her lung and liver, and she was facing a difficult prognosis and a lot of treatments. She was angry and frightened, and she cried. Everyone in the room cried. Then people started to yell advice from their own experience. They told her what had happened to them, how they had had the same prognosis and turned it around through a particular kind of therapy. They traded information. Have you seen this doctor, or tried this hospital? What was happening in the group was that everyone was saying, *"Don't give up."'* One man stood up and said that he had had a cancer that had begun with a huge tumor in his stomach. The doctors didn't want to operate on it because they felted he was terminal. He had one doctor who said, "Let's do it anyway." They did, and then he had to have many radiation treatments. His parents told him to be positive and to visualize being well. He was told by his doctors he had maybe two or three months because his cancer was so advanced. Then he said, "That was thirty years ago."

A chill went up my spine.

Betty, one of the group leaders, said that if the statistics say that only eight percent survive a particular cancer, nobody knows who the eight percent are. "Every one of us has just as much right to be in that eight percent as anybody else. If you have cancer," she said, "do everything possible to fight it—do any activity, any event, but participate in your recovery." She was given only a twenty-percent chance-eleven years before. It seemed like the room began to stir with hope.

About forty-five minutes into the meeting, Dr. Harold Benjamin appeared in the doorway. He is the founder and director of The Wellness Community. He is a Beverly Hills lawyer who started the Community with $250,000 of his own money in order to help cancer patients. He had always been interested in the dynamics of group therapy and had a five-year involvement as a "square" (non-drug user) in the controversial Synanon drug rehabilitation program. His wife is a long-term survivor of breast cancer and a sharing group leader active in The Wellness Community. He has written a book called *From Victim to Victor* that explains his philosophy about health, the principles of The Wellness Community. Harold is very charismatic. When he speaks, he does it with great humor and honest.

"The Wellness Community is not a place to come to learn to cope with having cancer or to die from it. It is a place to learn to participate in your fight for recovery along with your physician. We feel that if you participate in your fight for recovery, you will improve the quality of your life and just may enhance the possibility of your recovery. Your first line of defense against cancer is your own immune system. Scientific studies have shown that depression weakens the immune system—we are here to teach you the tools for the pursuit of happiness so you can be an active participant instead of a hopeless, helpless passive victim. . . .

"Please use us in any way you need and I hope everything turns out exactly as you would want."

He flaps his arms at us not to applaud, but it is difficult not to be impressed with his ideas and his passion about them.

One of my favorite people at the Wellness Community was a man named Jack. He is eight-five years old. He says he comes to The Wellness Community every Friday for an "emotional injection." He has his story down like a vaudeville routine. I adored him immediately because his jokes were right on the money and he always got his laugh. He had spinal cancer at eighty-three and was told he would never walk again. He was on chemotherapy in a pill form when I met him. He retaught himself how to walk with a walker, and then threw it away. He had a cane and threw that away. He says the only thing wrong now is he can't dance like he used to. He said to his doctors, "With the chemotherapy, how come I lost my hair?"

What he didn't tell his doctors was that he lost it fifty years ago. His wife, Sarah, is there with him. She helps if he forgets any of the jokes.

The first time I had to speak I was so nervous that I couldn't believe it. I didn't say my name, I just very quietly told about my cancer; I said that I was in treatment, that I had had some of my treatments already and that it was very difficult. I had a turban on my head. I thought I looked like an exotic African princess, but I was told later I looked more like Yasir Arafat. I was very shy and quiet about myself. But when other people talked and I saw their spirits falling low, I would yell something from across the room. Someone else would be on cisplatin and I would say, "I am on cisplatin, too. The side effects are rough, but six years ago when they didn't have it, we wouldn't have had any hope at all. Now we do!"

At the end of the two-hour meeting, which went by like a dream to me, I was just invigorated. I was so excited I couldn't wait to go back. I saw the beautiful woman stop crying and help someone else. I saw hope come into people's eyes. I couldn't shut up about it. I talked to Jodi the whole way home in the car. Gene was so worried that I would get depressed and instead I ended up driving everybody else crazy because I told every story that I heard there how it inspired me and how I couldn't wait to go back there again and how I wanted to lead the group and run the whole thing and I knew this was a great thing and I was onto something wonderful. Joanna kept saying, "Just relax. You can't *run* the thing, you *can't*. You are working on your own recovery. Just enjoy what you are able to do and how you can be helped by it."

Every Friday that I felt well I went back to the sharing group. That was my first step. For the first three times I never said my name or anything, and then one day I opened up and said, "My name is Gilda Radner and I am a performer by trade. When I got cancer it appeared on the cover of the *National Enquirer.* They said, 'Gilda Radner in Life-Death Struggle,' and ever since then everybody has thought I was dead. Well, I'm not dead—cancer doesn't have to mean you die."

Everyone in the room was looking at me a little more closely. It was as though at that moment I became Gild Radner. I got very funny as I told stories about going to a restaurant and seeing someone back up against the wall because he was so frightened to see me. "I don't know if he was upset because I was alive or because he didn't send me a card."

Suddenly, not only did have the room laughing, but I felt my thumb going up into the air like Rosanne Roseanndanna. There I was at The Wellness Community, and I was getting laughs about cancer and I was loving it. At the end of the meeting a lot of the women came up to me asking questions like "What kind of chemo are you on?" What happened when your hair fell out?" And I saw they were looking to me for answers or leadership. I tried to help and say what I felt. Then one of the women also said that she was a comedy writer and she had some material and would I read it—a three-hundred-page screenplay. But another woman who was there said, "Hey, look what she is going through right now—this maybe isn't the right time to bring that up."

The woman who wanted to give the material understood. It was wonderful because this other woman protected me, and I realized you just have to speak up say, "Don't cross this boundary." What happened in subsequent weeks was some kind of strange balance about being funny, being Gilda Radner, and being someone going through cancer. I found a way to tell my cancer story and get laughs from it. They started to use me for balance at the meetings after someone had told something really sad. They'd say, "Gilda, would you like to speak?"

Jack or I would come in to lift the room back up. I love to make people laugh, and at The Wellness Community I'd found my role again. It didn't matter there that I was Gilda Radner. It wasn't my reputation. It was who I was and who I always have been—someone who is funny.

from

Rosie O'Donnell:
Her True Story

by George Mair and Anna Green

MUCH of Rosie's childhood was shaped by her neighborhood, which was chock-full of other big Irish Catholic as well as Italian families. There were always plenty of kids around to play all sorts of games, starting with the Rockwellian basketball hoop over the O'Donnell garage. Rosie readily admits the influence of her brothers: "I was a tomboy—is that a shock to anyone? I didn't do ballet."

But she sure did sports. "I played softball, volleyball, kickball, tennis, and basketball; a regular tomboy jock girl and proud of it." Nor did she just play with the girls. "I was always the first girl picked for the neighborhood teams," she recalls with ill-concealed pride. "I got picked ahead of my three brothers, which I think still affects them. I always had time for a good game."

Rosie also managed to acquire a load of popular toys from the era—all of which she seems to still have. Rosie even swears she sent away for hordes of green plastic army men. She also played with her share of dolls, though many of them (Cher, Laurie Partridge, and the like) were collected more for their show business connections. Still, there was a bit of the nurturer lurking behind her tomboy exterior.

Commack in those years was a safe place for children to run riot on that best of all kid holidays—Halloween. And the O'Donnell kids had a trick of their own. Rosie and her siblings each took three masks when they went out, so that when they found a particularly noteworthy home—say one that dispensed full-size Hershey bars—they would run around the house, switch masks and voices, and return for second and third helpings. For Rosie, it was an early taste of theatrics, as well as an experience of chocolate abundance.

To any careful observer of the O'Donnell clan, it was clear that little Roseann was a ham waiting for a banquet. Her sister Maureen remembers her as a stand-up comedian almost before she could stand up. "Rosie was always telling jokes and doing imitations." One thing that made it easy for Rosie to develop a mimic's ear was her father's faint Irish brogue. Years later, she put that skill to good use, telling joke after joke at his expense, often exaggerating his accent.

Her stage debut came in the third-grade production of *The Wizard of Oz.* Around the O'Donnell home, acting out scenes from this classic tale was a happy pastime, except that Maureen always got to be Dorothy, and Rosie was assigned the role of the Mayor of Oz—no doubt due to her excellent ability to capture his distinctive voice. So in her own class, without her sister to compete with, Rosie desperately wanted to win the part of Dorothy. Instead she was cast as Glinda, the Good Witch, undoubtedly foiled again by her own talent. "Jan Brenner got to be Dorothy, and I never got over it. I remember it like it was yesterday," she said twenty-six years after the event. Years later, she wrote and performed her own parody of Oz in her stand-up act.

As the middle child of five, Rosie grabbed attention through her humor and her antics and quickly evolved into the classic class clown. She got away with lots of childhood pranks simply because she could fast-talk and jolly her way out of any situation. Gifted with a natural ability to entertain, little Roseann quickly became an ardent observer of the professionals.

While not all that interested in her studies at school, Rosie would have earned straight A's as a student of the performing arts. Television was ever present in her home, and as she recalls, "My whole family knew the entire fall schedule before it even went on the air. We had the *Newsday* supplement and we'd memorize what was on. We were a huge, huge, huge TV family.

Rosie grew up enchanted by such froth as *Gilligan's Island, I Dream of Jeannie,* and *Bewitched.* She was inspired by Marlo Thomas in the first feminist sitcom featuring a single career woman, *That Girl,* and later by her all-time favorite TV program, *The Mary Tyler Moore Show.*

Rosie's devotion to Mary knew no bounds. She dutifully kept a notebook about the show, and admitted years later that she might have been a tad compulsive: "I used to take notes all during the show, then copy them *over* into my MTM book. Can you say *therapy?*" Later she would review them again and again, as if for some cosmic pop quiz.

Though she learned early on that there was life beyond Commack, Rosie still drew inspiration from these shows about the possibilities that lay ahead for a girl on her own in the world. It was also the heyday of the prime-time variety shows hosted by the likes of Ed Sullivan, Red Skelton, and Jackie Gleason. Watching them, Rosie was exposed to every manner of entertainer from puppets to poodles, from the Beatles to Nat King Cole. But the variety performer Rosie most admired was Carol Burnett. She could dance, she could sing, she could act, she was funny—and she wasn't any typical Hollywood beauty. And Rosie wanted to grow up to be just like her.

One of Rosie's incentives to hurry home from school was an important ritual she shared with her mother—watching the cozy afternoon talk-variety shows put on by Mike Douglas and Merv Griffin. These easygoing guys presented the top talent of their day, from veterans to newcomers. Their shows served up true family fare—a long time before Sally or Jenny vied to book left-handed dentists who marry midgets. Mike Douglas even showcased their beloved Barbra Streisand for an entire week as his cohost. Rosie soaked it all up, every last detail, and stored it all away for another day.

Nor was young Roseann limited to daytime or early prime-time shows for her inspiration. She quickly became adept at overcoming her mother's best intentions. "My parents would make me go to bed, and I would sneak down and watch Johnny Carson from the stairs." And then she would tiptoe back upstairs and act out the role of talk show guest to her bathroom mirror. "I would say, as if I was thirty, 'You know, Johnny, when I was twelve, I used to sit in my bathroom and talk to you.'"

And though the O'Donnells were not a showbiz family, Roseann O'Donnell instilled in her daughter her own passion for entertainment of all kinds. "She was into musical theater," Rosie says of her mother, "and really nurtured that part of my life." One of the first Broadway cast albums Rosie memorized was *South Pacific.* Her favorite song from the show? "Happy Talk." Those are vivid memories for Rosie, the good memories she wants to keep alive. "I'd listen to *Oklahoma* over and over, and I'd wait every year for *The Sound of Music* and *Mary Poppins* to come on television." Rosie was the kind of youngster who sang show tunes for Show and Tell. "Other kids are bringing in Barbie dolls, and I'm singing *Oklahoma!*" she recalls.

There was no contest when it came to picking their favorite Broadway performer—Barbra Streisand won that honor by unanimous vote. In fact, Roseann O'Donnell arranged her family's schedule around events such as a Streisand TV special or the release of a new album or movie. Rosie sees 1968 as a turning point in her life, because that's when the movie *Funny Girl* was released. Even at the age of six, Rosie knew that when she saw Barbra up on that screen, it reflected exactly what she wanted to do with her own life. It was almost as if the family had their own set of holidays and observances dictated not by the Holy Roman See, but by Hollywood. And great mimic that she was, young Roseann could soon do every Streisand song she heard, all in Barbra's distinctive Brooklynese.

"I'd go into the kitchen singing 'Second Hand Rose' with Barbra's accent, and my mother would laugh and laugh," Rosie remembers. "It was a great way to get attention, so I kept it up." And so her mother became her first, and forever favorite, fan. Soon her mom was calling in the neighbors to enjoy her talented daughter, giving her an even bigger audience.

Even though their finances were sometimes strained, the O'Donnells exposed their budding star to as much entertainment as the budget would allow. Rosie remembers seeing her first musical when she was just six years old—a production of *George M* at the Westbury Music Fair in Long Island. These firsts were important to her, as they seemed to imprint her with another aspect of her vision for herself. At the same venue, Rosie also attended her first concert, performed by the Carpenters. Karen Carpenter was unique. In addition to singing, she did double duty as the group's drummer. She inspired Rosie to take up drumming in the family garage. To this day Rosie still plays a fast set of traps. She remembers the concert well, especially the part afterward when she stood around waiting for an up-close glimpse of her new role model. Suddenly Karen Carpenter passed by her—and "I reached through the fence and touched her sweater. It was like a big thing for me."

Looking at Rosie's fifth-grade class picture there is no portent of the tragedy to come. It shows a totally normal little dark-haired girl, captured in happy innocence. Yet all that was about to change forever.

Rosie's fondest childhood memory is sharing lemon drops with her mother in the third balcony of Radio City Music Hall. This is a gigantic theater, full of gilded splendor, one where a little girl could easily fall in love with the glamorous stage production that preceded the film. The Rockettes, in all their high-kicking, leggy perfection. A hall that resounded with live music from the spectacular pipe organ must have inspired young Roseann with more reverence than any church could ever have. This was her cathedral. A place to confess her deepest yearnings. A place with a movie screen so large she could lose herself completely to the story. To the illusions. To the magic. In the darkened theater, sitting safely next to her mother who understood such things, any dream seemed attainable to the starstruck young girl.

Biographical Notes

Russell Baker (1925–   ) The winner of numerous prizes and awards, Baker's autobiographical writing has been praised for its humor and perception as well as its ability to portray the way Americans live during the twentieth century. A graduate of Johns Hopkins University, Baker's career in journalism has ranged from the crime beat in Baltimore to chief of the London Bureau. The author and editor of more than 15 books, he is a regular contributor to many magazines and newspapers, including The New York Times.

Luther Standing Bear (1860s–1939) The son of an Oglala Sioux chief, Standing Bear had a unique perspective derived from his experience in the 19th century Native American culture and the 20th century white world. Standing Bear's writings are an eloquent preservation of Sioux l history, folklore and myths.

Rose Blue (1931–   ) Rose Blue is the author or co-author of more than fifty books for young readers. Her writing explores problems in the family such as divorce and alcoholism, as well as larger issues in society like racism and violence. Blue is also a popular writer of song lyrics.

Natalie Bober (1930–   ) Natalie Bober's goal as an author is to enable readers to hear the voices and experience the lives of her subjects. She wants young people to feel at home in another time and identify with heroine Abigail Adams—her triumphs and tragedies, her hopes and happiness. Bober began her prize-winning writing career during a long convalescence from a leg injury and published her first book, a biography of poet William Wordsworth, after it had been rejected by twenty-one publishers. She believes that persistence is a quality she shares with her subjects.

Michael Dorris (1945–1997) One of the most influential promoters of Native American studies, Dorris was part Modoc Indian, and won a prize for his Guide to Research on North American Indians, one of several top honors he received for his fiction and nonfiction. The Broken Chord: A Father's Story, an autobiographical study of fetal alcohol syndrome, was a widely praised book and television movie.

Doris Kearns Goodwin (1943–   ) Kearns Goodwin's best-selling biography of Franklin and Eleanor Roosevelt, *No Ordinary*

Time, won a Pulitzer Prize. A historian who has taught at Harvard, Kearns Goodwin is also an expert on baseball. She frequently appears as a guest on television talk shows, where she comments on history, baseball, and current events. She lives in Cambridge, Massachusetts, with her speechwriter husband and their three sons.

Stephen Hawking (1942–   ) After his graduation from Oxford University in 1962, Hawking was diagnosed with Lou Gehrig's Disease, a crippling illness that has confined him to a wheelchair and deprived him of speech. In spite of this handicap, he is admired as one of the most brilliant physicists of the twentieth century. A Brief History of Time, his exploration of the origins of the universe, has been translated into 40 languages and has made Hawking a multimillionaire. Still, he insists that "work is my relaxation."

Dan Jansen with Jack McCallum (1960–   ) Proclaimed one of the greatest skaters of the decade, Jansen's personal problems kept him from victory in two successive Olympics. Then on a bleak day in 1994, hours after his beloved sister died of cancer, Jansen overcame tragedy to win the gold and set a world's record in speed-skating. Sports Illustrated senior writer Jack McCallum helped Jansen tell his dramatic story. McCallum is also co-author of Shaq Attack!

Kathleen Krull (1952–   ) This talented author and editor has published a variety of books for children and young adults. While serving as a teacher at the University of Wisconsin, she has also brought out a series of young children's books as well as the prize-winning young adult work, Sometimes My Mom Drinks Too Much.

Bill Littlefield (1948–   ) A popular sportscaster for National Public Radio, Littlefield graduated from Yale University and teaches at Curry in Massachusetts. Although his first love is writing biography and other nonfiction, Littlefield's first novel, Prospect was praised by The Los Angeles Times as "wise and warm."

Eileen Lucas (1956–   ) Born in Chicago, Lucas is the daughter of a commercial artist. Because she is the mother of two children, she is deeply concerned about the world they will inherit. As a result, she writes and illustrates personally meaningful books for young people of all ages.

Nelson Mandela (1918–) He renounced his title as the son of an African tribal chief to become a political revolutionary against apartheid (state-instituted racial segregation) in his native South Africa. Jailed for twenty-six years, Mandela's fight for freedom ended in victory in 1990 when he was released from prison. He shared the 1993 Nobel Peace prize with South African president F. W. de Klerk for their successful struggle to bring nonracial democracy to their homeland. Like many other black South Africans, Mandela voted for the first time in 1994, in the election that brought him the presidency of the country.

Willie Morris (1934–) Born in Jackson, Mississippi, Morris's writing is rooted in the American South, but he has a keen and broad vision of the way people's lives are lived throughout the country. Morris earned a BA and MA from Oxford University which he attended on the prestigious Rhodes Scholarship. His writing has taken him from Texas to New York to Washington, DC.

Corinne Naden (1930–) The author or co-author of more than thirty books, Naden has always been fascinated by nonfiction because she loves the thrill of learning something new.

Mary Helen Ponce (–) Born in Pacoima, California, Mary Helen Ponce's writing has been translated into several languages, and she is as well known in Mexico as she is in the United States. She holds a Ph.D. in American Studies, loves to run and hike in the foothills of the San Gabriel Mountains, and is looking forward to buying a trail bike. The mother of four children, she also has two cats, Ramses II and Nefertari I.

Dot Richardson (1961–) Dot Richardson cracked the first home run ever in Olympic softball competition and overnight became one of the hottest stars of the 1996 games. Richardson, also an orthopedic surgeon, was an all-around athlete who focused on softball during her college career at UCLA. She got her start when she was ten years old, when a man who saw her playing invited her to play on a Little League team but told her she would have to cut her hair very short and go by the name of Bob—in other words, pretend to be a boy.

Gene Schoor (1921–) For more than fifty years, Schoor has been writing about winners in the sports world, an arena he knows and loves. He was a collegiate boxing champ who reached the finals of the 1936 Olympics. And, while continuing to coach, Schoor has served as author or editor on 38 books.

Nancy Shore (1960–   ) A former drama critic for *Stages Magazine*, Nancy Shore has also been an editor at several literary agencies, and her articles have appeared in *Art and Artists*. Among her recent publications are a biography of 17th-century reformer Anne Hutchinson and a book about the Spice Girls.

Gary Soto (1952–   ) Born to Mexican-American parents in Fresno, California, Soto is a multitalented writer who has published prize-winning poetry, short stories, novels and essays. Besides Aztec dance and karate, he also enjoys reading, traveling, and eating.

Don Yeager (1962–   ) A frequent collaborator on nonfiction books, Yeager has managed to merge his love of sports with his writing.

Acknowledgments *(continued from p. ii)*

Facts on File, Inc.
"Aung San Suu Kyi: Icon of Hope for Burma" from *Contemporary Human Rights Activists* by Eileen Lucas. Copyright 1997 by Eileen Lucas. Reprinted by permission of Facts on File, Inc.

Harcourt Brace & Company
"Blintzes Stuffed With Cheese" from *Lives of the Writers: Comedies, Tragedies (And What The Neighbors Thought)*, copyright © 1994 by Kathleen Krull, reprinted by permission of Harcourt Brace & Company.

HarperCollins Publishers
"Pen Pals" from *Paper Trail* by Michael Dorris. Copyright © 1994 by Michael Dorris. All rights reserved. Reprinted by permission of HarperCollins Publishers.

Kensington Books, an imprint of Kensington Publishing Corp.
"Because You're A Girl" is reprinted by permission from *Living the Dream* by Dot Richardson with Don Yaeger. Copyright © 1997 by Dorothy Richardson with Don Yaeger. Published by Kensington Books, an imprint of Kensington Publishing Corp. Reprinted by permission of the publisher.

Little, Brown & Company
From *Long Walk to Freedom* by Nelson Mandela. Copyright © 1994 by Nelson Rolihlahla Mandela. "Susan Butcher" from *Champions: Stories of Ten Remarkable Athletes* by Bill Littlefield. Copyright © 1993 by Bill Littlefield (text); Copyright © 1993 by Bernie Fuchs (illustrations). Reprinted by permission of Little, Brown & Company.

Wiliam Morrow & Company
"The Crown" from *The Good Times* by Russell Baker. Copyright © 1989 by Russell Baker. Copyright © 1989 by Russell Baker. Reprinted by permission of William Morrow & Company.

Pocket Books, a Division of Simon & Schuster
Reprinted with the permission of Pocket Books, a Division of Simon & Schuster from *Challengers: The Inspiring Life Stories of the Seven Brave Astronauts of Shuttle Mission 51-L* by the staff of the Washington Post. Copyright 1986 by The Washington Post.

Random House, Inc.
"A Faded Photograph" from *My Dog Skip* by Willie Morris. Copyright © 1995 by Willie Morris. Reprinted by permission of Random House, Inc.

Simon & Schuster
From *Wait Till Next Year* by Doris Kearns Goodwin. Copyright © 1997 by Blithedale Productions. From *It's Always Something* by Gilda Radner. Copyright © 1989 by Gilda Radner; renewed 1990 by The Estate of Gilda Radner. Reprinted by permission of Simon & Schuster.

University of Nebraska Press
"At Last I Kill a Buffalo" is reprinted from *My Indian Boyhood* by Luther Standing Bear by permission of the University of Nebraska Press. Copyright 1931 by Luther Standing Bear. Copyright © renewed 1959 by May M. Jones.

University of New Mexico Press
"La Familia" from *Hoyte Street: An Autobiography* by Mary Helen Ponce. Copyright © 1993 by the University of New Mexico Press. Reprinted by permission of University of New Mexico Press.

University Press of New England
Gary Soto, "The Bike" from *A Summer Life*. Copyright © 1990 by University Press of New England. Reprinted by permission of University Press of New England.

Villard Books, a division of Random House, Inc.
From *Full Circle: an Autobiography* by Dan Jansen. Copyright © 1994 by Dan Jansen. Reprinted by permission of Villard Books, a division of Random House, Inc.